marketing
that matters

10 PRACTICES TO
PROFIT YOUR BUSINESS
AND CHANGE THE WORLD

Chip Conley
Eric Friedenwald-Fishman

BK

BERRETT-KOEHLER PUBLISHERS, INC.
San Francisco

Berrett-Koehler Publishers, Inc.
235 Montgomery Street, Suite 650
San Francisco, CA 94104-2916
Tel: (415) 288-0260   Fax: (415) 362-2512   www.bkconnection.com

Ordering Information
Quantity sales. Special discounts are available on quantity purchases by corporations, associations, and others. For details, contact the "Special Sales Department" at the Berrett-Koehler address above.
Individual sales. Berrett-Koehler publications are available through most bookstores. They can also be ordered directly from Berrett-Koehler: Tel: (800) 929-2929; Fax: (802) 864-7626; http://www.bkconnection.com.
Orders for college textbook/course adoption use. Please contact Berrett-Koehler: Tel: (800) 929-2929; Fax: (802) 864-7626.
Orders by U.S. trade bookstores and wholesalers. Please contact Publishers Group West, 1700 Fourth Street, Berkeley, CA 94710. Tel: (510) 528-1444; Fax (510) 528-3444.

Berrett-Koehler and the BK logo are registered trademarks of Berrett-Koehler Publishers, Inc.

Printed in the United States of America

Berrett-Koehler books are printed on long-lasting acid-free paper.

Library of Congress Cataloging-in-Publication Data
Conley, Chip.
 Marketing that matters : 10 practices to profit your business &
change the world / by Chip Conley and Eric Friedenwald-Fishman.
 p. cm.—(The social venture network series)
 Includes index.
 ISBN-10: 1-57675-383-2; ISBN-13: 978-1-57675-383-5 (pbk.)
 1. Social marketing. 2. Social responsibility of business. I. Friedenwald-Fishman, Eric,
1966- II. Title. III. Series.
 HF5414.C66 2006
 658.8—dc22   2006008841

FIRST EDITION
11 10 09 08 07 06   10 9 8 7 6 5 4 3 2 1

About the Paper in This Book
The pages of this book are printed on New Leaf EcoBook 50 paper. This paper is made from 100 percent recycled fiber, 50 percent of which is recycled from postconsumer waste, and it is processed chlorine free. New Leaf calculates that compared with printing on virgin paper, printing 5,000 copies of this book saves twenty-four fully grown trees, 8,546 gallons of water, 15 million BTUs of energy, 1,115 pounds of solid waste, and 1,912 pounds of greenhouse gases. These calculations are based on research done by Environmental Defense and other members of the Paper Task Force. New Leaf Paper can be reached at www.newleafpaper.com or (888) 989-5323.

*Is it nurture or is it nature? In Chip's case,
his sense of social responsibility is
deeply rooted in what he's
learned from his parents,
Fran and Steve Conley.*

*Eric dedicates this book to his
parents, Paul and Sherry Fishman,
who demonstrate that ethics,
vision, and love always win.*

Contents

Letter from the Editor of the Social Venture Network Series

If you think marketing is nothing but advertising and promotion, Chip Conley and Eric Friedenwald-Fishman will set you straight in this remarkably concise and practical little book. For example, consider this astonishing fact (plucked from the introduction): "With annual sales of more than $125 million, [Chip Conley's company] Joie de Vivre spends less than $50,000 annually on traditional advertising yet has a greater market share than its hotel competitors."

Take a short trip through these pages, and Chip and Eric will show you how a values-driven approach to marketing can help your business increase profits, gain greater market share, and help you live a richer and more rewarding life.

As you might guess, this book does not advocate your grandfather's concept of marketing. *Marketing That Matters* sets forth a thoroughly contemporary approach to marketing that is fully in tune with today's intensely competitive and fast-changing business environment—an approach that will help you position yourself and your company for continuing success in the challenging years ahead.

The numerous examples in this book, drawn from the collective experience of companies affiliated with Social Venture Network (SVN) and from the authors' nearly four decades of experience with their own and other firms, illustrate how values-driven companies can succeed in the marketplace while helping make the world better. As Chip and Eric show so clearly, marketing truly succeeds only when it is an authentic expression of a company's mission and when it embodies the company's brand, expressing what they call "the three Vs: the value, values, and voice of an organization."

Marketing is at the heart of the success of a great many SVN-linked companies. As mission-driven firms, our businesses take naturally to the holistic approach to marketing espoused by Chip and Eric. That explains both why we are bringing out this volume on marketing so soon after the inauguration of the SVN series and why we recruited Chip and Eric to tell the tale.

Chip Conley's Joie de Vivre hospitality chain is a classic marketing success story and an ideal example of how values-driven marketing, honestly and persistently pursued, can propel a business into a commanding position in the marketplace. Similarly, Eric Friedenwald-Fishman's marketing firm, Metropolitan Group, shows dramatically how marketing rooted in just and humane values can win the day, not just for the company's dozens of corporate and nonprofit clients, but also for the company itself.

If you're looking for insight and practical advice about how to navigate the swirling waters at the intersection of market and meaning, you'll find them in this book. This pint-sized volume contains a gallon's worth of wisdom. You'll want to keep it on your desk and refer to it again and again. Enjoy!

MAL WARWICK
Berkeley, California
August 2006

Acknowledgments

This book would not be possible without the generous support of many people and organizations.

Chip acknowledges Debra Amador, my Wonder Woman, who was part editor, part researcher, part marketing consultant, and part taskmaster. She also introduced me to the pleasures of tea, and I treasure the friendship that has grown out of this project. Thanks to the Joie de Vivre team for giving me the time and space to indulge in writing, especially Rachel Carlton, who has taught me the true value of an executive assistant. Big hugs to my best friend and muse, Vanda Marlow, who's twice the writer I'll ever be. Hugs and kisses to my partner, Donald Graves, who suffered through me writing two books while he was toiling away in his anesthesiology residency. My fortunate involvement in this project was inspired by some savvy salesmanship by Deb Nelson at Social Venture Network, whom I adore, and by Johanna Vondeling of Berrett-Koehler who's as insightful as anyone I know in the publishing field. What would I do without Eric Friedenwald-Fishman, my coauthor? I learned so much from him in the process of writing this book and really appreciate his humanity and knowledge of this subject matter. Two last thank yous: one to Paul Hawken, whose book *Growing a Business* helped me see that there was another way to nurture my business; and, finally, thanks to Abraham Maslow, whose theories on human motivation have helped me understand how to create an actualized workplace.

Eric acknowledges Rebecca Friedenwald-Fishman for loving support, brainstorming, editing, and assisting in every way;

Maximilian and Sophie Friedenwald-Fishman and Naomi Fishman for patience; Hailey Stern for research support; Laura K. Lee Dellinger for edits and comments; Carole Leonhardt, the world's most organized assistant for everything, every day; Lee Collinge, Martha Wagner, and LeAnn Locher for ideas, brainstorming research, editing, and proofreading; the entire Metropolitan Group team for walking the talk; Brian Rohter and the team at New Seasons Market for inspiration; Jean Pogge and Joleen Spencer and the entire team at ShoreBank for ideas and support; the SVN community for ideas and vision; Geoff Fishman, Wendy Radmacher-Willis, John Donovan, and Mark Albion for words of support and wisdom; Richard Steckel, Jim Armstrong, John Drummond, Stan Amy, and Peter Hutchinson for pioneering work; my coauthor, Chip Conley, for smarts, spirit, and teamwork; all of Metropolitan Group's clients from whom I have learned so much; the wonderful companies who have shared their stories for this book; our supportive editorial director Johanna Vondeling, Berrett-Koehler, and Social Venture Network for sponsoring the series; the other series authors who are creating a wonderful body of knowledge; Kevin Lynch who had used the term "marketing that matters" and helped build awareness for socially responsible marketing. And to all social entrepreneurs who use their economic power to create a more just and equitable world.

Finally, we both want to acknowledge a company we learned about after brainstorming the title for the book. While there is no affiliation between the organization Marketing that Matters (a marketing strategy consultancy based in Seattle, Washington) and the authors or the content of this book, we wish to thank Zia Gipson, president and owner of Marketing that Matters, for kindly permitting us to use the phrase for the title of this book.

Why marketing matters

> If a traditional marketing campaign is really well done it makes people say, "Great ads. I like those ads." Values-led marketing evokes a different reaction. People say, "Great company. I love that company." Which response is likely to foster a more long-lasting relationship?
>
> BEN COHEN AND JERRY GREENFIELD, *BEN & JERRY'S DOUBLE-DIP: LEAD WITH YOUR VALUES AND MAKE MONEY, TOO*

Marketing is about creating relationships. Yet people don't want to be *marketed to*—they want to build a *relationship* with. A core question every company should ask itself is, "What kind of relationship am I building with my customers?"

Old-school marketing was based upon selling products or services. If you were a marketing executive and your company was launching a new product, you would call in your ad agency, look for a sexy or manipulative way to gain some "mindshare" from your target audience, and then spend the big bucks to sell your audience on why they should want your product. The relationship between company and customer would be purely transactional—not to dismiss the fact that loyalty sometimes would be created in the process.

New-school marketing is based upon satisfying needs. It recognizes that we live in a world of advertising pollution. Pushing product doesn't work anymore, especially in the era of the Internet, when savvy customers can connect with each other and trade stories about your product—and your company—and can easily find alternative choices. Furthermore, it isn't even all that clear who your target customer is anymore since traditional demographics are no longer so predictable, and traditional barriers such as distance have all but disappeared.

In the past, the company controlled the relationship, but in today's remote control world, customers are no longer passive. In fact, customers have never been so powerful. And after years of being manipulatively marketed to, customers have a healthy skepticism about most companies. And right they should.

During the last four decades, Americans have had cause to be skeptical of all of our traditional institutions, from government to religion to media to business. These institutions have not been consistently trustworthy. So the newly powerful customer, who still desires and searches for deeper relationships and meaning, looks for new institutions to fill the values vacuum.

Fortunately, the emergence of a whole new type of company—the socially responsible business (SRB)—has been one of the most promising commercial developments of the post-Vietnam era. More mainstream Fortune 500 companies are realizing that they can do well by *doing good*. When we write about socially responsible businesses in the book, we mean to cast a wide net as it's remarkable how many businesspeople in small and big companies are determined to create an intersection of market and meaning in their business. Certainly, a growing number of customers are altering their buying habits to assure they buy from companies that speak to their values.

Socially responsible business leaders recognize that for-profit companies have a massive impact on the world and as a result have responsibilities beyond maximizing return for shareholders. These leaders do their best to balance their company's need for a fair profit with the environmental and social needs of the community and their employees. In essence, socially responsible businesses look at their relationship with their community as being long-term and sustainable—not short-term and transactional.

Ask a few socially responsible entrepreneurs what "sustain-ability" means to them and you're likely to hear some very progressive ideas about how businesses can do a better job of taking care of the world. But they can incorporate environmentally and socially sustainable practices only if they have an operating model that allows them to sustain their business. Unfortunately, for many of these business leaders, marketing is seen as the ugly side of that operating model, a necessary evil when you realize that your bottom line isn't able to sustain all of your aspirational business ideals.

Quite often, entrepreneurs passionately pursue a new business idea and launch their new product or service to the world with all the enthusiasm of a small child making their first mud pie. Too often, entrepreneurs are disappointed when they come to realize that, outside of their circle of friends, no one has ever heard of them or their company. Rather than feel victimized by this reality, entrepreneurs who truly want to build a sustainable business need to learn the ABCs of marketing and how these apply to their unique business. That's where we come in. The voice of this book comes from two down-to-earth (or at least that's how we like to think of ourselves) entrepreneurs who've applied these marketing practices to our own businesses and have had the good fortune to glean wisdom from our contemporaries in a variety of industries. The culmination of these experiences is presented here to help you find greater success in your endeavors through socially responsible marketing, whether you're working for a green start-up or you're part of the marketing department of a multinational corporation.

Chip started Joie de Vivre Hospitality nearly twenty years ago and has grown it into one of the largest independent hotel companies in the United States, operating more than thirty-five unique hospitality businesses. As CEO, Chip has helped the company win a number of national awards, including the Guerrilla

Marketer of the Year, the Hospitality Humanitarian award, and the Experience Stager of the Year. Named as one of the Top 10 Companies to Work For in the Bay Area by the *San Francisco Business Times*,[1] Joie de Vivre has one of the lowest annual employee turnover rates in the industry (25 percent versus the hospitality national average of 75–100 percent) and consistently receives the highest marks for customer satisfaction. With annual sales of more than $125 million, Joie de Vivre spends less than $50,000 annually on traditional advertising yet has a greater market share than its hotel competitors.

Seventeen years ago, Eric founded Metropolitan Group, one of the country's leading full-service strategic communications and social marketing agencies, with offices in Portland, Chicago and Washington, D.C. As creative director/president, Eric has developed brands and marketing strategies for many well-known socially responsible businesses, has developed corporate social responsibility (CSR) and community engagement strategies for large corporations, and has been a leader in applying strategic marketing to the needs of nonprofits and public agencies. Eric's work has won national awards including the Public Relations Society of America Silver Anvil Award. Last year, the brand Eric helped create for ShoreBank Corporation was recognized by *Fast Company* as one of the nation's top ten storytelling brands.[2] Eric is particularly passionate about harnessing marketing to drive social change and is the primary author of the Public Will Building Framework, a model for approaching strategic communication to creating sustainable social change.

We both describe our companies as socially responsible organizations. By this we mean that our goal is to operate our companies to be profitable, great places to work, and positive contributors to our communities and the planet. We recognize that our own companies are constantly striving to improve and have found that marketing is an important part of this discussion. But that doesn't mean we're perfect. And you don't have to be either. Becoming a socially responsible business is a process.

We know some of you are involved with a small start-up and others may be part of the marketing department of a big company. While we haven't had the opportunity to interview each one of you about why you picked up this book, we believe you're looking for the following information from *Marketing That Matters:*

- How to build your confidence in the marketing arena so that you can understand what's worked and what hasn't for big and small socially responsible businesses.
- Language that can help you make your argument for why marketing is important to your business and how social responsibility can (and should) be factored in.
- An understanding of the core applications that you can use in your business, with specific tips for how you can immediately start using these practices.
- Inspiration from successful stories of businesses that have used the practices in this book.

Marketing That Matters is meant to be an easy-to-use field manual that you can refer to when you're deep in the trenches and looking for some direction. For those of you entrepreneurs who are sweating to meet payroll, we truly can relate as we've been there too. We're thrilled we can share these practices with you as hopefully they will help you grow revenues. Growing revenues has a miraculous affect on your ability to sleep at night.

We are not doctrinaire in our marketing belief system. Nor do we proclaim to hold the secret formula for marketing all socially responsible businesses. We believe the ten practices we'll introduce in this book are relevant to just about any company, but they are particularly useful to a company that's building a values-driven relationship with its customers. We do our best not to be righteous in our presentation of these practices because we don't think that's a particularly useful means of marketing— from us to you or from you to your customers. Furthermore, we may surprise you with some of our marketing philosophies. For example, we believe that it's okay to market a lifestyle and it's just fine to try to connect emotionally with your customer. Taking that approach to your marketing doesn't make you socially irresponsible, but it does mean that you can be on a slippery slope so you just need to be conscious about how authentic and open you are in your communications with your customers.

Three subjects get us on our soapbox, and we'd like to clarify them right up front. The first is the use of the word *consumer*. We don't use it in the book except when it's in a quote from someone else. If I approach you as a *consumer*, that makes me a *producer*, and neither one of those words sounds particularly humane or relationship oriented. In fact, one of the chief complaints of capitalism is that it creates consumers who are unconscious of the impact of their consuming. So you won't see us use that word as it dehumanizes the relationship and creates the opposite of what an SRB is looking to do: satisfy needs and desires rather than promote consumption.

Second, while we're big believers in pushing the envelope with marketing practices, we're cautious about how SRBs can sometimes handcuff their own organizations. For example, we've seen SRBs with poor marketing campaigns that came about as a result of choosing process over impact. What we mean by this is that they were so tied to their dos (always include all the facts and details, spend your advertising dollars only in publications that support your politics and point of view, only market products and services that are critical to human survival, etc.) and don'ts (never print in full color, never use humor in your marketing, etc.) that they forgot to ask, "Does this marketing approach have an impact on our customer?"

You will find that we see socially responsible marketing as inclusive of many techniques and practices that work for any business. Some provide SRBs with special advantages because they are better suited to carry them out and to be believed. Others require additional caution for SRBs because we can be held to a higher standard.

Finally, we get on a soapbox about narrowly defining marketing as a set of promotional tactics (advertising, PR, etc.). You will find that we see marketing as a broader business strategy that informs numerous choices critical to establishing, building, and maintaining customer relationships. We believe this is especially true for socially responsible businesses. So in this book about marketing, you will find us discussing human resources, supply chain, product development, and customer service strategies and examples because we see them as imperative to walking the talk of real strategic marketing.

Chapter 1 outlines our belief that marketing is a core part of business strategy. It's not something you do purely to promote a product or service or to trumpet the philanthropic efforts of the company (although that can be an important part of a marketing strategy). Instead, developing a marketing strategy, along with tactics that introduce your product to your ideal customer, is one of the true basic foundations of business and is part of making key operations and management decisions.

Chapter 2 will help you delve a little deeper into the core mission of your company. We provide you with a list of key questions and tips that will help you clarify your value proposition, your values, your voice, and, ultimately, the soul of your business.

Chapter 3 adds a little accountability measure to the mix by way of asking, "What is your definition of success?" We introduce a matrix that will help you think about your advancement of mission versus your return on investment. Most importantly, we amplify our belief that defining clear goals is an essential part of developing and executing a successful marketing plan.

In the next few chapters, we ask you to explore your relationship with your customers. Chapter 4 will help you become more aggressively customer centered by learning your audience's needs, desires, values, and perspectives. Whether you're creating an organizing principle for understanding your customer, encouraging your customer to help create the product, or tapping into listening posts to clarify how your customer feels about your company, we firmly believe that building a close relationship with your customers is one of the best steps you can take for your business.

Chapter 5 asks you to question conventional wisdom, something that may come naturally to socially responsible businesspeople but could be missed when they focus too much on "preaching to the choir." We ask you to evaluate your assumptions about your market—are you just preaching (or marketing) to the choir or have you imagined how your product or service can reach out to a wider audience? This is an important chapter because many entrepreneurs make the mistake of creating a product purely for themselves without considering how a few tweaks in their product or marketing could help them reach untapped markets.

Chapter 6 is required reading for any business with a desire to become more socially responsible and create a deeper relationship with their customers. This chapter explores the classic question, "Are my customers choosing my product or service because they like the tangible value it provides them or are they choosing it because they like the values that we're espousing?" SRBs are faced with a balancing act between communicating value and values to their core customers *and* communicating them to their secondary customers. Get this right, and your customers will love you. Get it wrong and they're likely to ignore you.

We know that chapter 7 may bother some of you because our basic premise is that it's important to connect with your customers' hearts first and minds second. That premise is part of the reason many of us are disgusted with manipulative mainstream advertising. Yet to ignore human nature may make you righteous, but it won't necessarily make your business sustainable. This chapter explores how you can build a relationship with your customers by developing a brand story and an authentic voice. We will dispel the notion that SRB customers would prefer to wade through walls of statistics in a crowded marketplace. For most of our customers, emotions trump data.

Once you know your audience and have opened yourself to a broader market, communicated value and values, and connected emotionally with your core customers, it's time to empower your customers to be messengers for your product. Chapter 8 is all about building community to support grassroots, word-of-mouth marketing. This chapter will highlight the impact of trusted advisors, show you opportunities to build community around a brand, and amplify the importance of empowering employees, customers, and strategic partners to be effective messengers.

We finish the book with one cautionary chapter and one inspirational chapter. Chapter 9 espouses that authenticity is the bedrock upon which the marketing of an SRB is built and transparency is the insurance that keeps it on solid ground. This chapter demonstrates the importance of ethics and alignment with mission and brand promise in day-to-day operations of a business and across all business relationships. SRBs are held to a higher standard than most other companies. It's essential to be cognizant that you operate under a microscope, not just being watched by your customers and the community but also by your employees. SRBs have an opportunity to create a distinctive relationship with customers based upon trust that comes from creating authentic experiences and authentic marketing. They must walk the talk. Do you?

Finally, we finish with chapter 10, which suggests that business can be a platform for changing the world. Businesses have powerful voices and extensive reach. The communication and marketing tools that engage employees, customers, and community members offer a unique opportunity for businesses to leverage the power of their voice to effect positive social change. This chapter explores how your product can directly serve as the message for social change and how your marketing can amplify voices for change, and it gives you techniques to empower customers and communities in these efforts. You will read some powerfully inspirational examples of businesses that have not only helped change their industries but have also helped change the world.

Throughout these chapters, you will read numerous examples of socially responsible businesses from all sorts of industries— from adventure clothing and gear (Patagonia) to household supplies (Seventh Generation), and from children's toys (Wild Planet Toys) to socially responsible banks (ShoreBank). Some of these businesses may be familiar to you; many may not. We also point out examples of large and mainstream corporations using these practices to demonstrate their potential scale and broader use. We mix in our own companies' experiences where we can add personal perspective and to illustrate that the practices also work for service businesses. We hope that using a diversity of examples from various industries, regions, and sizes of companies will give most of you the chance to see your own needs reflected.

We also thought it would be helpful for you to see how one company uses each of these practices. So in each chapter you will find a serial case study featuring a Portland-based company called New Seasons Market. We selected New Seasons because it is a great example of each practice, because it is relevant to readers with large and small companies (New Seasons is a mid-size company with over one thousand employees that was a start-up just five years ago), and, in the spirit of full disclosure, because Eric knows New Seasons' leadership well and has worked with their employees on their marketing.

Upon finishing this book, we hope you will have a new appreciation for how marketing is an integrated and holistic part of any business enterprise. We hope that you will take the ideas that are shared and scale their use to your own needs. For some of you, that will mean developing detailed strategies based upon the ten practices. For others, it will simply be asking yourself some of the questions we illustrate that can help you make better choices.

Marketing is truly about creating relationships. But for SRBs this is about more than just the quantity of interactions with the customer. What is essential is the quality of those interactions, which help to build relationships that result in friends for life. We hope that you can use the information and ideas in this book to build meaningful customer and stakeholder relationships. We believe you can benefit your business and positively impact the world by leveraging *Marketing That Matters*.

Don't fear marketing

PRACTICE 1: USE MARKETING
AS A CORE BUSINESS STRATEGY

"Marketing is just smoke and mirrors."

"It's all about selling people things they don't need at prices they can't afford."

"Marketing uses slick ads and exploitative tactics to take advantage of stereotypes, fears, and unrealistic fantasies."

"No one but large corporations can afford it."

"Unless you have a sophisticated marketing department, an ad firm, a PR agency, and millions of dollars, don't even bother with marketing."

"We're not ready for marketing. Once we have finalized the product, worked out the bugs, and seen how it works, then we might invest in it."

We've all heard and, at times, hidden behind these myths. Marketing is often seen either as a shady practice—not appropriate for a socially responsible business—or as a mysterious and expensive luxury that few companies can afford. Clearly, you are not a true adherent to either of these beliefs or you would not be reading this book—or maybe you're just curious. In any case, while many examples of marketing are not being used in either an ethical or an effective manner (and the same can be said for accounting, law, human resources, information technology and any other business function), solid marketing is a key component of business success that can support both the financial and social bottom lines of your organization. But to make sure we're all on the same playing field, and to take the mystery out of the word, let's take a few moments to talk about the term.

Many people use the term *marketing* to refer to a broad set of promotional and outreach activities aimed at communicating a business proposition to customers and other important audiences. These activities often include advertising, media relations, direct mail, promotional offers, online promotions, sales materials, and other marketing tactics. While all of these tactics are important applications of marketing (and many will be referred to as practical approaches in later chapters of this book), it is the definition of marketing as a strategy—or strategic marketing—that is our primary focus.

Strategic marketing is acquiring a deep understanding of the needs and desires of your existing and potential customers and designing your business (products, services, delivery mechanisms, customer experience, branding, outreach, etc.) to meet and exceed their needs and desires. When energy bar leader Clif Bar developed the Luna bar, the core idea for creating the product—active women need an energy bar and have different nutritional needs than men—was a demonstration of the pure definition of strategic marketing. The strategic marketing decision to design an energy bar specifically for active women then led to many other strategic and tactical choices regarding product design, branding and packaging, product distribution, community partnerships and, ultimately, promotional and sales strategies.[1]

At its core, good strategic marketing can be deeply aligned with building a socially responsible business because it demands a constant focus on the customer's needs, drives development of quality products and services, and often encourages alignment with customer values. Thus, the first practice of *Marketing That Matters* is simply to use marketing as a core business strategy.

The practice of using marketing as a core business strategy really boils down to defining and utilizing marketing as a central function of *business planning* within your organization. Thinking about marketing as a baseline of business development and ensuring that marketing-based questions and analyses are present and utilized in all business planning processes, makes marketing an integrated business strategy. Rather than mapping out the product concept, price point, manufacturing and distribution plan and then asking, "How will we sell it?" adherents to this practice ask, "How do we design the product concept, set the price, et cetera, to best meet the needs of the market?" This is a hallmark of a customer-centered marketing approach. Just think about the repackaging of single servings of yogurt so that they no longer require a spoon. By putting yogurt in a tube and making it more convenient as an on-the-go snack, companies developed a product that responded to a need of busy parents—healthy snacks they could pack in a lunch box or send on a play-date with no muss or fuss.

Core Applications

We have identified three applications of using marketing as a core business strategy to help integrate this practice into your business:

1. Make sure that marketing is "at the table" from the beginning.
2. Distinguish between strategy and tactics.
3. Develop and use marketing plans.

Make Sure That Marketing Is "At the Table" from the Beginning

In some companies, marketing efforts are orchestrated by a dedicated marketing professional. In many others, marketing is executed from the corner of an entrepreneur's desk and competes with all other business needs for his or her time and attention. Regardless of the capacity and sophistication of your marketing resources, making sure that the marketing mind-set is at the table from the beginning of each major business decision—and throughout the development process of a company, product, or service—will help you avoid pitfalls, expand opportunity, and drive success. This requires broadening your view of the tasks you define as marketing—from designing for the market from the beginning of your development process to figuring out how to sell once the development process is complete.

Silk has become a leading soy beverage brand and helped define the soy milk market because the product was designed to align with customers' habits and desires. Silk used the marketing perspective of understanding customers to make key strategic choices about how to position the product in the store and in customers' minds. Customers were used to grabbing a half-gallon of milk in a carton with an angled top from the supermarket dairy case rather than hunting for a flattop box in the health food aisles. Silk's marketing choices included the package design (just like a traditional milk carton), distribution strategy (at mainstream grocery stores), and in-store location (in the dairy case next to the milk).[2]

To help establish the marketing mind-set, we have filled this book with suggestions of the questions and perspectives that need to be at the table. Each practice we outline in chapters 2 through 10 will help you integrate a marketing point of view into the life of your business. If you do nothing else after reading this book, make sure that someone in your company is assigned to take a marketing perspective and to ask tough questions at every key business meeting. This will enable you to make better choices and help you advance your business goals.

Distinguish between Strategy and Tactics

Many marketing efforts do not maximize and leverage resources because they invest in marketing tactics before establishing a marketing strategy. Similar to purchasing Sheetrock, pipes, and windows prior to developing a design concept and blueprint for your home, focusing on what your ad will look like before identifying your priority audience and your core value proposition creates waste, inefficiency, and missed opportunities. Marketing strategy encompasses the development of clear goals, identification of the audiences or customers who must take action to achieve these goals, understanding of the core product or service proposition that meets audiences' needs and desires, and development of key emotional and intellectual messages needed to move the audiences to action. Marketing tactics are the means or tools that deliver the messages to the audiences.

Since marketing tactics are more tangible than strategies, many companies naturally jump first to thinking about—and at times even developing—an ad, media release, brochure, Web site, or other promotional tactic before establishing a strategic framework that helps them identify which tactics will deliver the greatest return on investment.

Keep the following points in mind to help distinguish between strategies and tactics:

Marketing Strategies	Marketing Tactics
Identification of measurable goals and objectives	Direct outreach (employee and customer communication, customer experience, design, etc.)
Understanding of audience needs, desires, values, options, etc. (see chapters 4 and 5 for more detail)	Collateral material/print presence (packaging, brochures, sales sheets, etc.)
Segmentation and prioritization of audiences	Online communication (Web site, viral marketing, etc.)
Development of core business, product, or service proposition	Advertising (print, electronic, online, out of home, etc.)
Identification of your outreach approach (e.g., engage true believers, demonstrate the lifestyle, link to community values, etc.)	Public relations (media relations, community relations, public affairs)
Selection of tactics to implement your approach (see list in right hand column)	Promotions (contests, events, discounts and incentives, etc.)

ColorGraphics in Seattle is one of a small number of print-ers on the West Coast that is certified by the Forest Stewardship Council (FSC). It utilizes rigid water and air quality standards, careful paper use planning, and fast-drying UV inks that emit fewer toxins—all of which reduces its impact on the environment and produces a higher-quality print product. ColorGraphics wanted to create a brochure to better sell its "green printing" advantage. But prior to developing the brochure, the leadership took a step back and asked, "Who are our current customers and our desired customers, and why will they select us?" They conducted executive interviews with print buyers and CSR managers, learning that their company's potential customers thought of green printing merely as using recycled paper and considered price and quality as the main decision drivers.

ColorGraphics learned that it needed to educate the market about green printing and get the "better quality" message up front: its green printing process wasn't just environmentally responsible, it was of better quality. The leadership team decided to create a marketing strategy that defined their message framework, segmented their audiences, and served as a guide for the development of a brochure and identification of other tactics that would effectively educate the market. ColorGraphics began its process by determining the need for a new brochure (a tactic) and moved to addressing the need to educate the market about green printing and refining its message (strategies).[3]

Very often, clients' first communication with Eric's agency will be to declare that they need a brochure. Eric's agency then asks the following questions:

- What business goal is the brochure designed to advance?
- Who are the target audiences?
- What do we need them to do?
- What do they need to know in order to take the action we want?
- How will they get the brochure?
- How will we get them to read it?

Once clients hear these questions, it often becomes clear that a strategy, and not a brochure, is the first need. A marketing strategy answers the first question of whether a brochure is the right tool and then, if it is, how it should be designed. Whether you are driven by saving trees, saving money, or seeing a return on your marketing investment, asking *why* every time you say or hear, "We need a _____ ," will ensure a better bang for your buck.

So each time you're in a meeting and discussion of a tactic begins, ask yourself or your team, "Is this effort based upon, and in accord with, our marketing strategy?" If it isn't, or if there is not a strategy in place, capture the good ideas about tactics and set them aside while identifying your strategy. You can then return to the tactical ideas, develop those that advance your strategy, and discard those that do not. In short, never do tactics before strategy.

Develop and Use Marketing Plans

A simple discipline to ensure that marketing is a core business strategy, and that strategic marketing is driving tactical choices, is to use a written marketing plan or framework for every major initiative (business launch, product or service extension, new market launch, etc.). The act of writing down your plan demands that you ask and answer core marketing questions. This produces more informed choices and makes it easier to communicate your strategy to other team members and partners.

Before succumbing to the myth that marketing can be done only by those with deep technical knowledge and big budgets, keep in mind that marketing plans can be tailored to fit the resources and market potential of each venture or individual project. A marketing plan developed to roll out a new menu for a single-location restaurant and a plan developed to roll out a national product will justify significantly different levels of time and resource investment. However, both plans ask the same fundamental questions. Whether written on the back of a napkin and pinned to your bulletin board or developed by a multi-disciplinary marketing team and presented to your investors, taking the essential step to clearly define your proposition, and the strategy to connect it with the market, helps drive good decision making and effective marketing. While every business benefits from this kind of planning, we have found that many socially responsible businesses shy away from it. So grab your napkin or your laptop and ask a few basic questions:

- What are our business's mission and vision?
- What measurable goals do we need to accomplish and advance our mission and vision?
- What market needs/desires are we seeking to fulfill?
- What customer/audience segments are we targeting?
- What do we know about each segment's needs, desires, relevant habits and behaviors, communications and media preferences, and core values?
- What is our compelling market and value proposition (the unique benefit customers receive in exchange for their purchase)?
- What is our compelling values proposition (the unique social benefit customers create/share by voting with their dollars)?
- What are the key messages (emotional and factual) that are critical to motivate action by our target customers/audience segments?
- What are the most effective marketing tactics to deliver the message to customer/audience segments?
- How much do we need to invest in time and money to be effective?
- Who needs to be responsible for each task and what are their deadlines?
- How will we measure success?

In the following chapters, we will look at practices that further define, illustrate, and answer these questions.

ShoreBank Corporation is the nation's first and leading community development bank holding company. It operates banks in Chicago, Cleveland, Detroit, and the Pacific Northwest and offers consulting services around the world. ShoreBank pioneered the combining of socially responsible deposit accounts with lending that develops affordable housing, invests in minority-owned businesses, and funds green building and environmental projects. After nearly thirty years of business, the bank saw a need to refresh its brand and make it better known. What began as a brand development process soon identified the need for a strategic communication plan and a more consistent and strategic approach to marketing.

ShoreBank answered the list of marketing questions referred to above, learned a great deal about its customers and potential customers, and developed a strategic communication plan. The plan put in place a more customer-centered approach to designing marketing materials, the bank's Web site, and public relations activities. It also called for the creation of a marketing planning worksheet that helps managers ask strategic questions as they develop their marketing tactics. And the plan helped ShoreBank make the decision to redefine its marketing department and to hire a marketing strategist to lead the team and also serve as an internal consultant and coach to managers across the company.[4] Mary Houghton, one of the four founders and president of ShoreBank Corporation, sees firsthand the changes that the strategy has created, "We started investing in marketing strategy and management capacity and there is now constant attention to marketing with solid pay-offs."[5]

Remember, there is value to writing down a plan. The process of asking and answering the questions listed above and the act of committing your plan to paper (or to an electronic document) will force you to make better choices, create a road map to guide your marketing efforts, and help you get more value from your investment of time and money.

USING MARKETING AS A CORE BUSINESS STRATEGY

New Seasons Market was founded in 2000 by three families in Portland, Oregon. They now have six stores, with three new locations under construction, and over one thousand employees. In *Grist Magazine*, natural business trailblazer Paul Hawken highlighted the importance of stores committed to supporting the regional food economy and used New Seasons as an example, "To me the company that is exemplary is the New Seasons Market in Portland, Oregon. They buy everything they can locally. These are real community food stores with wonderful food and fresh produce and fish. They know the purveyors. They talk about them. They really feed and enhance the local food web of Oregon and Southern Washington and Northern California. They are to me your model of what a grocery store can do to help farmers and citizens and communities."

In developing the concept for New Seasons Market, the founders looked at the audience of health-conscious customers and foodies and at the larger audience of weekly grocery shoppers. They realized that an unmet need existed to provide great natural and organic foods, plus incredible quality and variety, along with the basic groceries that most families buy and the shopping convenience that most families need. They knew that beyond the true believer market of deep green customers and galloping gourmets, there existed a much larger market looking for organic produce and Frosted Flakes for their kids, the finest balsamic vinegar and Diet Coke, the option to be socially responsible with their grocery budget and stop at just one store for their weekly shopping. An efficient checkout line and the chance to get some cooking advice and meet local farmers would also appeal to these shoppers. In other words, there was a golden opportunity for a value proposition that combined quality, convenience, and experience. Brian Rohter, one of New Seasons Market's founders and its CEO, describes developing the model: "It was important to create a shopping experience that was familiar and viewed as the neighborhood store and not some natural foods Mecca or oasis. We recognized that most people don't just eat natural foods. When we go to friends' houses and open the refrigerator we also see Diet Coke, and presliced cheese for their kids' sandwiches. We thought that people should be able to get it all in one shopping trip—ultimately, eat and let eat."[6]

In developing the business plan, store designs, inventory mix, brand identity, and staffing and service model, the New Seasons team kept a marketing perspective for telling the story at the table for each planning meeting. This effort included recruiting a core team of people who met around the kitchen table to specifically play this role.

New Seasons put a priority focus on developing overarching marketing strategies before making decisions about the supporting tactics. A few of the key strategies included

- Developing a brand that firmly positioned the company as a primary grocery store and a store for everyone—"The ultimate neighborhood grocery store"—rather than a specialty, natural foods, or alternative store.
- Designing the in-store customer experience to "walk the talk" and using this as a primary marketing vehicle, which includes a staffing model and customer service focus that will provide customers with a comfortable, fun, and easy shopping experience.

- Providing health, nutrition, environmental, and socially responsible messages as opportunities for customer discovery, rather than using prescriptive and judgment-based orders.
- Developing a marketing plan format for planning sessions and then turning it into a simple document for each store opening, product rollout, or major initiative.

According to Brian, "Telling the story about what we do and why we do it is as important as how we do it. People have lots of choices about where to shop for groceries and our job from the beginning was to let them know we were doing things in a different way. I remembered all of the shops I have seen with great stuff inside and friendly staff, but not one customer—because they didn't take the storytelling side seriously."[7] From day one, New Seasons Market embraced—rather than feared—marketing.[8]

Don't Fear Marketing

Strategic marketing is not a prescribed set of tactics. It is not a veil of spin to push products or services. It is not a mysterious and Byzantine faith to be practiced only by an anointed few. It is a focus and a discipline that helps you understand the needs and desires of the marketplace and make strategic choices that effectively leverage your resources. Strategic marketing drives success by connecting customers with your answers to their needs. A business that offers the best product or service in the world is great only if it responds to real needs and meets customer desires, and even then it's great only if customers know it exists. Strategic marketing does more than move product. It also positions your brand, advances your causes, and creates real relationships with your customers. Strategic marketing drives success for all the bottom lines of your business—particularly your goals for social responsibility.

Now let's delve a little deeper into the core mission of your company and explore ways to clarify your value proposition, your values, your voice, and the soul of your business.

Know yourself

PRACTICE 2: BUILD UPON YOUR MISSION

Most of you reading this book picked it up either because you are part of a mission-driven organization or because you want to make your organization more mission driven. You are likely part of a group referred to as "true believers" because of your deep passion for both the core work of your business and the way you manage your business to help create positive social impact that extends beyond the financial bottom line. Your passion for your mission has the potential to be put to work as a marketing practice and to help differentiate your business. In the last chapter, we showed you that the belief that marketing and mission-driven business practices are incompatible is a myth. In this chapter, we will explore the power of a clear mission and the importance of using it as a decision-making tool for marketing. We will explore how to develop, nurture, and build equity for a strong brand.

An excellent example of a company building a brand and delivering on its mission promise to the customer is New Leaf Paper. New Leaf is a leading producer of paper made from 100 percent postconsumer waste (all content has been recaptured after being used and recycled). As its mission, New Leaf seeks both to deliver a quality product to the marketplace and to change customer and community expectations. It promises "to inspire—through our success—a fundamental shift toward environmental responsibility in the paper industry." New Leaf's mission drives its marketing goals to increase market demand for its product, while its marketing success advances the company's mission to change the paper industry.

To help drive this revolution in the paper industry, New Leaf's Eco-Audit program shows how many fully grown trees, gallons of water, Btus of energy, pounds of solid waste and greenhouse gasses were saved with each order printed on its paper. Its customers, ranging from ShoreBank to the Gap, print New Leaf's Eco-Audit trademark on their materials to help demonstrate their own commitment to the environment and, in the process, become brand ambassadors for New Leaf. Many graphic designers recommend New Leaf to their customers because of this value-added feature, extending the reach of the New Leaf message to create what serves as a volunteer sales force for New Leaf. The company's logo (a piece of paper with a corner folded over to reveal a leaf on the other side) conveys the link between its product and a healthy environment, and it conveys the message of market transformation that is at the heart of New Leaf's business strategy.[1]

Another excellent example of brand building and effective mission delivery is Stonyfield Farm. The company mission consists of the following: to provide a product of the highest quality; to educate consumers and food producers about the value of protecting the environment and support family dairy farmers to stay independent and adopt sustainable farming methods; to serve as a role model of a business that can be environmentally and socially responsible as well as profitable; to provide a healthy, productive work environment; and to provide an excellent return on investment to stockholders and lenders. The brand's early focus on the importance of organic food and its tagline "For a healthy planet," along with Stonyfield's customer education programs, helped build the organic yogurt category and establish a high-value organic dairy industry. Stonyfield's marketing and mission success has allowed the company to garner a major market share of the overall American yogurt market.[2] Building upon a mission and establishing a strong brand create a virtuous circle: the more you do one, the more you are able to do the other.

Core Applications

To help you move in the direction of New Leaf Paper and Stonyfield Farm, we have identified two applications you can use to help integrate the "build upon your mission" practice into your business:

1. Clarify your mission and live it.
2. Build a strong brand and live it.

Clarify Your Mission and Live It

While you may know in your gut what your organization's mission is and whether the choices you are making are in sync with it, many businesses lack a clear mission statement, have a mission statement that is outdated, or have their mission in writing but do not see it manifested in the day-to-day operations of their organization. If we were to review the mission statements of a handful of businesses, we would find a broad range of approaches—from comprehensive tomes that outline in detail what the organization does, to vision statements connected with strategic objectives, to philosophical constructs that delve into the metaphysics of commerce.

In fact, many of the strong mission-driven clients that Eric's firm has worked with find that while founders or senior leaders are very clear on their mission, this clarity is not always evident companywide. When asked about the mission as part of a brand or marketing audit, a significant number of line staff and managers either do not know their organization's mission, or they define it in such a broad way that it is nearly unrecognizable. If an organization isn't clear about its own mission, you can be certain that customers won't be either. Decisions about how the company operates, communicates with customers, and delivers its products or services will be equally inconsistent. While this is true for any business, socially responsible businesses have a heightened responsibility to make their mission real and use it to drive both operations and marketing decisions.

To make your mission statement a living and powerful marketing and business asset, you need to think of it as we do: as the expression of the soul of your business. Your mission is the long-term, big-picture reason for your existence. When you look at your value and values proposition, your mission should answer the question why. *A powerful mission statement articulates the core of what an organization does and the aspirational and often audacious outcome that the organization is pursuing.* We find that single sentence mission statements, written for both internal and external audiences, are easier for people within an organization to remember and are much more powerful as marketing tools. You can always convey additional information as a vision statement, philosophy outline, or operating principles. *But keep your mission statement short in length and big in vision.*

An excellent example of mission clarification is shown in the work of Chicago-based ShoreBank Corporation. ShoreBank has been America's leading community development bank from the time of its founding in 1973. As the organization grew, its focus expanded to encompass the link between environmental and economic well-being. The bank realized it needed an updated mission statement that was reflective of both the community development and environmental focus and was inspirational and easy for employees of numerous affiliate companies to identify with and remember. The new mission statement, "ShoreBank invests in people and communities to create environmental health and economic equity," became the core organizing principle of the bank's new brand and a central message delivered across the entire organization.[3] Ron Grzywinski, ShoreBank's chairman and one of its four founders, credits the new mission with helping the whole organization understand their roles. "The words of our new mission are so strong—they really make a lasting impression. In our recent all-employee survey, 89 percent of our employees agree that they understand how their job relates to the mission, which is a major improvement. They understand the links between ShoreBank's community development and environmental missions. Clearly, the brand and increased strategic communication get credit for this change."[4] Infusing the mission statement into employee recruitment, orientation and training, product and business development, customer relationships, and marketing messages has helped ShoreBank differentiate itself from the competition and grow its market share.

A strong mission, however, is much more than just a statement or an easy-to-remember slogan. In fact, if you stop there, you won't realize the full value at all. A strong mission is a tool you can and should use to make decisions that support a socially responsible brand. Using the question, "How does this choice advance our mission?" and demanding defensible answers from your teams—and from yourself—will facilitate better decision making and create a stronger basis from which to communicate with your employees, customers, suppliers, the media, and, ultimately, the marketplace. In fact, you ideally want to transform all these audiences into messengers and ambassadors for your brand. To do that well, it is vital that you build a connection between each of them and a mission they can believe in—and one that resonates with their own values. (We will go into greater depth about the power of people as messengers and ambassadors in chapter 8.)

To keep your mission front and center, we offer the following tips:

- *Examine it.* Even if it is relatively new, are you sure that it feels right and that everyone knows it?
- *Talk about it.* When making major decisions, planning a marketing campaign, or designing a new product or service, include your mission in the discussion. At the beginning of major projects (strategic planning, brand development, marketing strategy development), find out whether people are on the same page about the mission. Ask your team, "What is our mission and how do you use it?" Review the mission statement and ask if it answers the questions, "Why do we exist?" and "What will be better if we are successful?"
- *Out it.* Make sure your mission is easy to bump into and easy for others to hold you accountable for delivering. Put it on your Web site, post it in your facilities, and print it (where possible) on your materials. Engage your employees, customers, and suppliers by telling the story of your mission.
- *Live it.* By integrating the mission into the daily operations of your organization, you empower managers and staff to walk the talk and customers to experience your mission.

Build a Strong Brand and Live It

If the mission is the heart and soul of your business, then the brand is the voice and personality. Every organization has a brand. Some brands are designed deliberately and some occur without planning. Some of you think of branding, like marketing, as a charged word. It is thought of as natural beauty by some and cosmetic surgery by others. We define brand as an authentic expression of an organization. *A brand is the aggregate experience that audiences (customers, suppliers, employees, shareholders, stakeholders, and communities) have of an organization.* It is the embodiment of what we call the three Vs: the value, values, and voice of an organization.

Great brands, like great mission statements, reflect the true essence of an organization's mission, culture, and the delivery of promise. Great socially responsible brands are aspirational in their reach. They push those who encounter them to participate in something bigger than the gratification of their own needs—they are world changing. It is imperative that the market's tangible experience of an organization rings true to the brand and, at the same time, the brand helps stretch an organization to advance and grow. While any brand should have these attributes, socially responsible brands have a heightened responsibility for authenticity as a result of stakeholder expectations and the need to drive success to financial, social, and environmental bottom lines.

An excellent example of authenticity in branding is found in Tazo Tea. Tazo started as a very small company in Portland, Oregon. The brand is authentic in its focus on the journey one takes with tea, the clear connection to tea-growing regions and the tea growers, and how the drinking of tea makes the customer feel. The names of its teas reflect the experience of each flavor rather than the particular tea leaf. Calm for chamomile, Refresh for peppermint, Awake for English Breakfast, and so on. Tazo's brand is also aspirational—its packaging and brand voice convey a global presence and an appeal to the tea drinker's desire for adventure and discovery.[5]

As the Tazo example illustrates, brand is much more than a logo and a slogan. It's a story. It's a compass. It's a baseline that audiences identify with, see themselves as part of, and build loyalty to over time. Your brand helps connect audiences to your organization. It helps you make choices and prioritize marketing resources. It provides a launch pad for each effort that in turn leverages your other investments in marketing and the reputational value you have built for your organization.

An essential strategy to maximize all of your marketing resources is to establish a clear brand platform as the base from which you build all of your marketing strategies and tactics. As you make choices about how to market your product or organization, you should be asking, "Is this choice consistent with the brand platform?"

A strong brand platform includes these elements:

- Your mission statement—The expression of the soul of your business.
- Your brand statement—The essence of your brand and your core value proposition.
- Your core brand messages—The three to five lasting emotional or factual pieces of information that differentiate your organization.
- Your core values—The values that are fundamental to how your organization operates and is experienced.
- Your brand voice—The tone and personality of your organization.
- Your visual and audible identity—The name, logo, and tagline.

ShoreBank Corporation's new brand platform has been a successful component of the bank's growth. When ShoreBank was developing its new brand, it sought extensive input from leadership and staff from across the company and then invited current and potential customers to participate in focus groups. Customers said that ShoreBank's positive change message resonated deeply with them. However, they also said they felt like they were not included as part of the solution with the draft tagline "Change the World." In more than one focus group, a participant suggested involving the customer in the tagline by adding "Let's." ShoreBank now invites customers, businesses, and communities to partner with the bank in advancing a shared vision of healthy and vibrant communities. Every day, ShoreBank's brand issues the inclusive invitation "Let's change the world." Every day, thousands of depositors, neighborhood businesses, and community revitalization organizations say, "Yes, let's," and in partnership with ShoreBank, they do change the world.[6]

Great brands are developed through understanding the vision that you and your team hold for your business while also understanding the needs, desires, perceptions, and values of your audiences. As ShoreBank learned, to really know yourself you must understand what your customers and potential customers think of your organization, your industry, the products and services you offer, the position of your competitors, your role in the community, and the values relevant to their decisions about your business. Regardless of your marketing budget, finding opportunities to learn about audience perceptions in the process of designing or refreshing your brand and to engage external audiences in testing your brand will provide valuable feedback and a great return on investment. In chapter 4, "Know Your Audience," we provide more examples and tips on how to learn about and from your audiences.

Once you have defined your brand platform, you must use it. Going through the exercise of creating it will not help your marketing efforts unless, much like your mission statement, you use it as an integrated part of your operations. You must live the brand.

By consistently applying your brand, each marketing activity gets a boost from the equity already established by the brand,

and you can leverage other marketing initiatives, building additional equity for your brand. In every organization larger than one person, the laws of nature and the beauty of individualism ensure a dynamic tension between adhering to the brand guidelines and creating your own approach. While the entrepreneurial instinct and sense of ownership that a brand can inspire is a major strength, it can be even more effective if it takes advantage of and builds brand equity. So how do we create cultures in which brand application is the norm and in which the brand really belongs to everyone? Two imperatives to make your brand come alive and to maximize its impact are

- Make it easy. Make it easy for staff to apply the brand rather than develop stand-alone messages, materials, and approaches.
- Make it mine. Establish your brand as everyone's brand instead of just the marketing department's or leadership's brand.

Make It Easy

Carrots work much better than sticks when aiming for brand consistency. The most frequent reason that brands get diluted is that well-meaning staff and managers lack the tools they need to communicate, or they're stymied by perceived or real marketing bureaucracies. By establishing clear and easy-to-use brand guidelines, and accessible pathways for assistance and review, you make the consistent application of your brand much more likely. Building and making available flexible and easy-to-customize branded tools (PowerPoint and ad templates, Web page templates, HTML e-mails, talking points, etc.) that meet the needs of frontline and management staff make using the brand easier. In developing brand implementation strategies for clients, Eric often finds that the largest brand consistency complaints (e.g., "Our staff is constantly making flyers that do not carry the brand.") are an indicator of which templates or easy-to-customize tools are needed.

Make It Mine

We often think of a company's leadership and marketing staff as being the guardians and messengers of the brand. But in reality, the brand belongs to everyone, and it is only fully effective when everyone walks the talk. How the phone is answered, how products are designed, how orders are fulfilled, how complaints are handled, how quality is managed, how services are delivered—each either supports or contradicts your brand promise. By making the brand real and personal for each member of your team, you invest in the most powerful means to build relationships with customers and communities. By investing in making sure your brand is owned across your company you are building the foundation for real and lasting brand equity.

Just because a brand has been developed on paper, is supported by leadership, and may even have guidelines and tools, one can't assume that the brand is part of an organization's culture. Good branding engages internal audiences as much as external audiences. After including your employees in the development of the brand platform itself, you need to roll out your clearly defined brand to your entire team. Every member of an organization needs to be seen as a brand ambassador and needs to know that this is expected of all employees in the company. To be effective in the brand ambassador role, all staff members will need training and tools to help them succeed.

Include brand training for all staff in any new brand roll-out and as part of new employee orientation. Make sure all employees get the opportunity to talk about the brand, to put the key messages into their own words, and to tell stories that convey the brand. Share the best stories that illustrate your brand—it is so much easier for people to remember and tell stories than to regurgitate slogans. Whenever new employees, members of the executive team, or branch managers are asked, "Where do you work?" and then, "What does your company do?" their easiest answer should be the core brand statement because they have had the chance to use it and to make it their own.

Build in natural systems to reinforce the brand. Consider establishing a brand champion in each department or business unit. The brand champion is an employee who gets a bit more training, receives frequent updates and success stories to share, and can be a resource to peers. Provide recognition to employees who exemplify the brand in their work, and publicize to your internal audiences examples of your brand helping your company achieve its economic, social, and environmental goals.

So remember to clarify your brand, to invest in building ownership of the brand across your team, and to integrate the brand into all marketing discussions to drive consistency.

NEW SEASONS MARKET

BUILDING UPON YOUR MISSION

New Seasons Market uses its mission and brand as compass points for making decisions that advance its values and strengthen its market position. Fundamental to its mission is supporting the regional food economy by sourcing local products wherever possible and highlighting the connection between rural producers and urban customers. Part of this effort involves repositioning food from being seen as a commodity, selected on the basis of price, to being seen as a handcrafted product selected on the basis of value. Connected to this aspect of New Seasons' mission is a core pillar of its brand: "Really local and really good."

New Seasons builds upon its mission and reinforces its brand across the organization. For years, before any law required it, New Seasons labeled where its produce, meat, and dairy products came from—often down to the actual farm.

Learning from small local farmers about the economic challenges they face from commodity pricing, New Seasons created a half-time merchandiser position to coordinate with farmers. This merchandiser places advance orders and provides purchasing projections so local farmers can plan ahead and get a fair price. This person also scouts for innovative and special produce that farmers are passionate about and brings unique offerings to New Seasons customers. New Seasons' Brian Rohter focuses on the personal connection and says, "We have become friends with many of the people who grow and raise the food we sell. The personal connection really motivates us to do the best we can to make sure that they get fair pay for the work they put into the food we all eat."[7] The fresh and local products mix is not the only way that New Seasons makes the urban-rural connection. Nearly every weekend, some of the region's farmers, ranchers, fishing boat captains, winemakers, and brewers visit the stores, sample their products, and visit with customers. They create relationships and increase customer knowledge of the area's delicious, nutritious, and specialty foods and beverages and the people who produce them.

To increase the number of value-added jobs in the regional economy, New Seasons also added another half-time position to help existing regional food and beverage manufacturers and entrepreneurs develop products that will be carried at New Seasons. And it established a partnership with the state of Oregon's Food Innovation Center to help small entrepreneurs get the technical assistance they need to get high-quality products to market.[8]

Every day, in every department, New Seasons Market is advancing its mission and building brand equity as the ultimate local grocery store. In media stories, comments on blogs, and discussions at office watercoolers, it's not uncommon to read or hear comments like "Why wouldn't you pay twenty-five cents more per pound to know that farmers are making a living, that your food is healthy, and that your tomato didn't contribute to global warming by flying across the world?" All good questions.

Know Yourself

A clear mission and a strong brand platform authentically inject marketing into the daily operations of your business and empower staff, strategic partners, and customers to serve as messengers. By inserting your mission into daily discussions and integrating your brand across the organization, you create a strong foundation upon which marketing strategies and tactics can be built to leverage each other and reinvest in your brand. Using these core aspects of your company's soul and identity as decision-making tools will help you make strategic choices that advance your mission, build your value, and align with your company's and your customers' values.

Now let's take a look at how you define and plan for success.

What is your definition of success?

PRACTICE 3: DEFINE YOUR GOALS

Smart businesses set tangible goals to guide their marketing strategies. They want to know which efforts are making a difference, if their dollars are being well spent, and how they can measure what works. Socially responsible businesses also want to know if they are making a difference in the world. Every business leader at some point asks, "What portion of my marketing dollars am I wasting?"

A more strategic view of the question is to ask, "How do I know that I am investing my marketing resources in a way that gets a return on investment?" You will note that our question asks about marketing *resources* rather than marketing *dollars.* This is because the actual investment in marketing is one of dollars and one of time, energy, and the focus of the people in your company. In this chapter, we explore the questions you can ask to set goals and some of the measures you can use to leverage your marketing efforts.

Before we get into a discussion of the many typical marketing measures, it is useful to step back and consider that one of the great opportunities you have is to determine what you are going to measure and to set goals based upon your business needs and values. In fact, the goals of socially responsible marketing often include a mix of traditional marketing and social impact measures. As we move through the discussion of goal definition, let's remember that advancing both your economic bottom line and your values are legitimate outcomes impacted by marketing.

A fundamental principle to start our thinking about goals is the truism "What you measure matters." Certainly, both of us in our businesses have found that when we proclaim that we really care about something, the ability to measure it, track it, and suitably reward its advancement makes our decision making much more strategic. This motivates our teams to focus. Before we delve into the rest of the chapter, here are a few examples from our own businesses.

In Chip's hotel company, customer satisfaction, customer suggestions, and customer experiences drive many of the business and marketing choices. It is feedback Chip's team measures and deeply values. His company works with an outside customer satisfaction measurement group that monitors daily feedback from Joie de Vivre's hotel guests. This group, Market Metrix (a San Rafael–based company that conducts customer and employee satisfaction surveys), has studied data on hotels around the world. It has found that one particular measurement, the guests' perception of employees' can-do attitude, is the number one determinant of whether the guests were happy with their hotel experience—and whether they'll return.

So, while Joie de Vivre reviews all of the fifty measurement tools Market Metrix uses, Chip and his company pay special attention to the can-do score and have, in fact, created a companywide goal. If the company can average a can-do score of ninety-two for one year (which is at the "world class" index level of the top tenth percentile in the world), then Chip and his two senior executives (who happen to be men) have to come to the next company holiday party dressed as the Supremes and sing "Ain't No Mountain High Enough." Throughout the year, Joie de Vivre reminds all of its employees of this goal and the fun payoff at year-end if they meet the goal. Even though seeing Chip and the gang in dresses is a good motivator, what is really important is setting a goal that will increase the number of return customers. So for Joie de Vivre, creating and measuring a goal for great customer service is actually a key marketing goal.

At Metropolitan Group, Eric identified that contract acquisition and average account size matters to the company's bottom line (a very traditional professional services marketing goal). However, this had not been measured as part of employee performance. When measures and rewards tied specifically to individual employee contract acquisition were added, there was a significant increase in new accounts, client renewals, and revenue. But there is more to the story. Eric and his team had refused to put this basic measure in place for nearly fifteen years because they felt it would undermine a core part of the socially responsible workplace ethos—the commitment to have a workplace that was a community. They had deep fears of creating internal competition and a "dis your neighbor" sales culture. So when they finally decided that they really needed to listen to the saying "What you measure matters" and put individual goals in place, they also launched a teamwork goal. On the same six-month time frame that new business bonuses are calculated, all employees complete a survey where they score each of their co-workers on a scale of 1 to 5 on four questions:

- Is he/she generous with his/her knowledge?
- Does he/she give credit where credit is due?

- Does he/she do what he/she says he/she will do?
- Is he/she willing to jump in to help others?

The top 10 percent of the teamwork scorers also receive a bonus—because at Metropolitan Group, teamwork and culture also matter. The result? The contract acquisition numbers (measured with comparative data) and the esprit de corps (measured with a confidential annual all-employee survey) have both significantly improved.

Now some of you may be asking what a teamwork goal has to do with marketing. The reason we view this as part of the marketing discussion is twofold. First, as we have discussed throughout the book, one issue for socially responsible businesses is a fear of marketing or a feeling that it is antithetical to social responsibility. Eric had that same fear but realized that socially responsible business leaders can set their own goals and their own rules. His epiphany: you could have sales goals and also motivate teamwork and community culture.

Second, for many service businesses like Eric's, the happiness of the employees and the workplace culture are critical parts of creating the customer experience that brings customers back and generates referrals. Customers are buying creative services (that rely on a team of professionals delivering a collaborative product) and trust in the expertise and mission-driven passion of Eric's team (which is directly connected to customers' experience and their relationships with the team). So Metropolitan Group is delivering on a value/values proposition—providing customers with a valuable service or product and delivering it in a way that values relationships and demonstrates commitment to the client's social mission. We will go into more depth about creating your value/values proposition in chapter 6.

While the sales goals linked to teamwork at Metropolitan Group met two of its bottom lines (economic and great place to work), the company determined it could radically influence its third bottom line—social and environmental impact. The team members again looked at the saying "What you measure matters" and determined that they needed to set impact goals and link them to new business development efforts. They established a set of priority customer segments that would impact the issues, people, and communities that advanced their mission of "crafting creative and strategic services that help social purpose organizations create a just and sustainable world." Metropolitan Group determined to exclusively focus on clients in the following segments: environment and sustainability; children, youth, and family well-being; libraries and education; social justice; community development; public health; arts and heritage; foundations; and socially responsible businesses. Before expending marketing resources, staff need to demonstrate that the targeted client is in one of these segments and that Metropolitan Group's work will either directly impact social change or build the client's capacity to impact social change. The company assigns annual contract dollar goals to each segment to assure that advancing its mission is meeting the company's economic bottom line. Metropolitan Group also captures impact data from clients to measure the social and environmental results of its work. By setting a marketing goal centered on social impact, Metropolitan Group is able to drive audience segmentation and revenue goals.

So what you measure matters. How your business identifies the key areas that you will measure makes a major difference in your marketing choices and how you gauge success. Setting tangible goals allows your business to prioritize resources, empowers employees to execute and adjust strategies, and allows you to be true to your core value/values proposition. By defining your own bottom lines and by designing your marketing approach to meet them, you can drive economic and mission results.

We have discussed ShoreBank's mission and brand in previous chapters but turn to it again here as an example of an organization that uses many of the traditional marketing and business measures that one would expect of a bank—return on equity, profitability, and increased market share. ShoreBank has also established and utilizes measures that are directly related to its social goal and advance its values proposition. For example, ShoreBank sets a goal of making sure that each year it delivers in development outputs (loans that fund community development projects in inner city neighborhoods) at least two times its equity capital. Ron Grzywinski explains, "Our monthly snapshot shows earnings, development outputs, and environmental outputs compared to the budget. All employee bonus plans require employees to perform on the social/environmental impacts and on earnings. Our goal is to have new development outputs to be at least two times capital—last year it was 3.9 and has been consistently above the benchmark."[1] ShoreBank's community development lending far exceeds the percentage of community development lending conducted by traditional banks to comply with the Community Reinvestment Act.[2]

Your business can design and implement your marketing to deliver value and values by blending the traditional value, profit, market share, and positioning goals that all companies should utilize in their marketing strategies, with your social, environmental, employee, and community relations goals.

Core Applications

We have identified three applications you can use to help integrate this practice into your business:

1. Clarify and codify your goals.
2. Identify your return on investment and advancement of mission expectations.
3. Reward and publicize the results that you value.

Clarify and Codify Your Goals

First, articulate your big-picture goals and the specific outcomes that will demonstrate those goals are being achieved. Clarifying your goals will help you establish the decision-making infrastructure for a marketing program that delivers strong business and social results. Then, develop measurement and tracking procedures for the advancement of your goals. Codifying your goals will create accountability and provide the tools to monitor success.

The following are examples of traditional marketing goals:

- Increases in market share—For example, the goal of Rugmark (an independent nonprofit that inspects and certifies rugs as child-labor free) is to increase the percentage of hand-tied carpets purchased in the United States that are certified child-labor free.[3]

- Comparative sales revenue growth (comparing time periods, locations, ratios to staffing, etc.)—For example, New Seasons' goal of increasing per-store weekly sales.[4]

- Market diversification (expanding geography, demographic reach, customer segment reach, etc.)—For example, New Leaf Paper's goal of garnering high-profile publishing and catalog accounts.[5]

- Increases or changes in distribution channels—For example, Joie de Vivre's goal of increasing the percentage of bookings through its own Web site.

- Improved positioning (often measured by awareness and brand recognition)—For example, ShoreBank's goal of increasing its name recognition and brand awareness in Chicago.[6]

Socially responsible businesses often articulate nontraditional marketing goals. Such goals can include social and environmental impacts, changes in purchasing behavior, and attitudinal changes among customers (use of alternative transportation, increased use of healthy foods, use of energy efficient products, etc.).

For example, Flexcar provides easy access to new, well-maintained cars in various urban areas. Flexcar serves people who either do not own a car or are making the choice to utilize alternative forms of transportation for many of their trip needs and need a car that they can rent by the hour, hassle free.

Flexcar's core and driving marketing goal is to increase the number of customers (members) using Flexcar and in so doing decrease individual dependency on auto ownership. The non-traditional part of this very traditional marketing goal is that each time Flexcar increases its customer base, people's reliance on owning a car—along with the ratio of perceived required autos per household—goes down. This ties directly to Flexcar's values proposition: create an alternative to the single-user auto culture and its negative impacts. Flexcar is trying to reduce the significant ratio of autos to people in urban areas, a ratio that translates into congestion on urban streets and significant carbon output into the atmosphere. The Flexcar alternative can positively impact quality of life and improve air quality.[7]

Clarifying your goals also drives innovation and changes in business strategy. The Swedish appliance company Electrolux, one of the world's largest home appliance makers, has taken a holistic approach to environmental management. When it realized that most of its environmental impact was in the use of its products (not in the manufacturing process), it established marketing goals to drive increased product efficiency. Electrolux measures the share and profitability of its total sales of environmental products compared to its conventional products.[8] To further reduce its environmental impact, Electrolux has begun an experiment of giving away washing machines and charging customers by the load of laundry to promote more energy- and water-efficient customer use.[9]

Part of codifying your goals is to make them measurable. Establishing measurable goals for your marketing initiatives will hold you and your marketing team accountable for the choices that you make and will provide you with valuable data to adjust and improve your strategies.

gDiapers, a company that brought the first flushable diaper to the United States, is creating a significant environmental benefit by preventing tons of disposable diapers from ending up in landfills and putting human waste where it belongs—in the toilet. gDiapers established both market share goals and a commensurate goal for a reduction in tons of disposable diapers going into landfills. Its three-year goals were made clear and simple to measure. gDiapers plans to garner 0.5 percent of the U.S. diaper market and prevent over ten thousand tons of disposable diapers from entering the nation's landfills.[10]

Regardless of the specific goals you set, what is important to take away from this application is to make a practice of setting solid goals. Make sure your goals are

- Specific—Clear statements that outline what will be achieved or what will be different.
- Written—Easily shared with others who will be responsible for implementation.
- Measurable—Able to track progress and build data that can be used for comparative purposes.
- Deadline driven—To help keep you and your team accountable.

Identify Your Return on Investment and Advancement of Mission Expectations

We've used the term *ROI,* or return on investment, and while we believe most of you already have a clear idea of that term, the jargon buster definition follows: return on investment is the aggregate impact (tangible return) to the company, business, or brand that is received in comparison to the amount of dollars invested in a particular marketing strategy or tactic.

A companion measure to return on investment is *AOM,* or advancement of mission. Advancement of mission is a way of creating benchmarks that demonstrate that the organization is advancing its mission, its values, or its social purpose in the world. The advancement of mission measures will be different for each business and often include both tangible and intangible returns. Ideally, the measures of AOM should be tangible, such as the number of calls made to congress via the socially responsible long distance service offered by Working Assets, and the amount of money raised to combat the environmental causes of breast cancer by Luna. ShoreBank, in the example above, linked an economic measure of loan production to advancing its mission of increasing the investment in underserved communities. In other words, as the amount of dollars invested in development loans increases, the availability of decent affordable housing, expansion of businesses that offer family-wage jobs, and the number of energy efficient buildings also increase in ShoreBank's communities. ShoreBank measures its advancement of mission by tracking its performance against development and environmental lending goals.[11]

A traditional marketing exercise for most businesses when designing marketing strategies is to identify their anticipated return on investment and establish a system for measuring their actual results. Once you have identified your potential strategies, take a step back and examine the potential investment (including hard costs and dedicated human resource costs) and the potential return (measured by revenues, the number of new customers, increasing account sizes, etc.) for each proposed marketing strategy. You can use the anticipated return on investment as a decision-making tool to select which strategies and tactics, out of a myriad of potential choices, offer the best investment of your time and money. For example, Eric's Metropolitan Group set and reached the goal of increasing its contract acquisition by 30 percent (about $1 million) in 2005. He budgeted and spent approximately $48,000 for the additional travel costs and billable staff time that was allocated to land the increased accounts. His return on investment was approximately $952,000.

Once the selected marketing program is launched, measuring and tracking the return on investment based upon the actual results data helps you make decisions to expand programs that work and to reduce or curtail programs that don't perform.

As you focus on growing an increasingly socially responsible business, we encourage you to add questions to your traditional ROI analysis that will help identify marketing choices that will advance your mission. Ask yourself these questions:

- Does this marketing strategy align with our values?
- How will this marketing strategy advance our mission?
- Does this marketing strategy create social value (due to the expansion of use of our product or our service) in ways that have a positive impact in the world?
- Does the selected marketing strategy help expand service offerings and product availability into underserved markets?
- Does the messaging or the delivery mechanism (advertising, PR, etc.) help convey a positive social message and/or support a social cause?

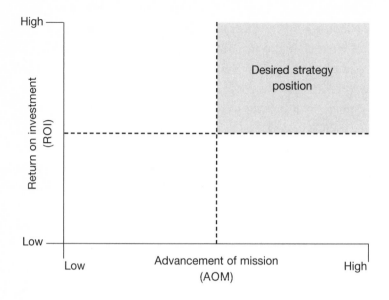

This chart illustrates the conceptual positioning of the ideal marketing strategies for socially responsible businesses. The horizontal axis is advancement of mission; the vertical axis indicates return on investment. Clearly, the "sweet spot" for a business marketing choice is in the upper right quadrant, where you have both high AOM and high ROI.

An example of a marketing tactic in this sweet spot is the weekly conference call for Warm Spirit. Warm Spirit is a natural body care products company whose customer base is primarily African American women. Warm Spirit's social mission is to empower African American women as entrepreneurs. The company's primary means of distribution, in addition to its catalog and Web site, is a large network of twenty thousand consultants or associates—independent businesswomen who sell Warm Spirit products. For 2005, Warm Spirit set an aggressive growth goal of reaching $10 million in sales. Its advancement of mission goal was to drive over $5 million in earnings to its network of consultants and develop the skills of these entrepreneurs. The goal was surpassed by over 40 percent.

Nadine Thompson, cofounder, CEO, and president of Warm Spirit, cites her weekly conference calls as the firm's most important marketing investment that has also served to advance its mission. Nadine hosts a conference call every Monday that is open and voluntary to Warm Spirit consultants. The calls include product and company information, but they also teach skills and build community. Training sessions are offered on using technology, developing sales skills, self-care and wellness, spirituality, and business ethics. Every week, three hundred to four hundred African American women call in from across the country and participate.

Warm Spirit receives terrific feedback from participants about the value and content of the calls. Since the calls are voluntary, recorded, and available 24/7 via phone and the Web, Warm Spirit uses the consistent live participation measure as its indicator that the community created on these calls is meaningful to its consultants. But it is the tangible measure—that 75 percent of the company's total sales comes from regular participants of the calls and that, as a result, Warm Spirit exceeded its stretch sales and revenue sharing goals—that indicates to Nadine the high ROI and tangible AOM from this program. So this marketing activity, which has a very low dollar cost and a relatively significant time and attention cost from senior leadership, results in an extremely high ROI (dramatically increased sales and continued engagement of the highest producers for the organization). And it provides significant AOM benefits (driving revenue to women entrepreneurs and strengthening a network that builds life and business skills for Warm Spirit's core constituency).[12]

Needless to say, few marketing strategies are a perfect blend or an equal measure of both ROI and AOM. Often the right choices will offer high return on investment and good advancement of mission, or high advancement of mission and a solid return on investment. The point is not to abide by some rule that all marketing choices and strategies of socially responsible businesses must fit in a particular quadrant of the chart. Rather, the point is to use this chart conceptually and ask yourself questions about ROI and AOM when you design strategy and evaluate results. If you do, you will make better choices to meet your combined goals.

Reward and Publicize the Results That You Value

A careful balance needs to be maintained when publicizing your company's business results, particularly your social responsibility results. Many organizations are rightfully cautious of communication that smacks of "green washing," or bragging or operating responsibly purely for the sake of image. At the same time, creating accountability for reaching your goals and sharing results with your shareholders, customers, employees, and community stakeholders can create a positive marketing and socially responsible impact. Making your goals and results known internally can motivate employees to achieve your marketing goals and create trust by reporting on your own accountability. Reporting externally can establish distinct market positioning, build trust with customers, and influence other businesses to adopt socially responsible practices.

When publicizing your results, identify which audiences make sense to communicate with on a case-by-case basis. Some goals may be appropriate to share with staff but may come across as spin to customers. Other goals can be shared with existing customers, in the form of additional information that reinforces their purchase choice, but are not appropriate for all stakeholders.

One of the factors that contributes to ShoreBank's positioning as a leading-edge "triple bottom line" company is its willingness to report its own progress toward mission performance.

ShoreBank profiles its development and conservation lending results and its profitability in internal updates, annual reports, online newsletters, and e-mail customer updates. This communication reinforces the choices that depositors and investors have made to do business with the company (as a customer, you receive a financial return and make a difference). Sharing achievement of its triple bottom line goals also provides a strong marketing platform to garner additional mission-based deposits and to strengthen ShoreBank's position as the leading community development bank in the United States and a preferred provider of community development consulting services on an international basis.[13]

gDiapers commits to its aggregate impact in terms of tons of diapers kept out of landfills and is creating a tool for customers to gain personal perspective on their environmental impact. The company is developing a Web-based calculator for parents so they can see the amount of waste their family will prevent from entering landfills by their choice to use flushable diapers.[14]

In chapter 2, we highlighted New Leaf Paper's eco-audit program, a strategy that publicizes the environmental results and fulfillment of environmental goals for each client. By providing specific data on the positive environmental benefits for each sale of its paper, New Leaf reinforces the choice its customers have made to use its paper and provides for its customers a powerful marketing message that publicizes their commitment to environmental sustainability.[15]

Many companies include traditional marketing measures of sales, increases in revenue, and acquisition of new accounts as part of their reward and performance accountability program. Companies that integrate social and environmental goals into their marketing and business strategies can make the rubber meet the road by including advancement of these goals in their employee reviews and reward systems.

As you make marketing decisions, remember that by publicizing and rewarding your marketing goals, you can drive the results you value.

Stonyfield Farm offers a terrific example of the results that can occur by integrating top-level strategic marketing and social change goals. Its focus on increasing market share for its brand and for organic yogurt has advanced hand in glove with its goal of increasing the economic viability and number of farms that use sustainable and organic practices. Stonyfield not only holds the dominant market share in organic yogurt (75 percent in 2005) but also is the fastest growing of all yogurt companies. It has significantly expanded the organic and environmentally sustainable dairy farming industry by building a supplier network of hundreds of farms, and it helps many conventional farmers convert to organic.[16] Clearly, what you measure matters.

NEW SEASONS MARKET

DEFINE YOUR GOALS

One of the marketing goals of prime importance to New Seasons Market is its positioning as the ultimate neighborhood grocery store. This overarching goal has direct correlation both to creating a primary grocery shopping relationship with customers (rather than a specialty shopping relationship) and to reinforcing its brand position as local, local, local. New Seasons takes its community involvement seriously for many reasons. Like many socially responsible businesses, its primary motivation is to be involved in its community and be a good neighbor because it is the right thing to do. But because New Seasons recognizes that what it measures matters, it has made a number of choices that have helped drive its positive impact in the community and has made significant contributions to achieving its ultimate neighborhood grocery store positioning.

New Seasons knew that being a good neighbor requires more than writing a few checks. It recognized that it could leverage the large concentrations of neighborhood shoppers who view shopping at the store as an asset to raise money for community needs and to connect people with causes that are important to their neighbors. Enter the Benefit BBQ. Throughout the year, New Seasons partners with nonprofits that are important to the community. It produces benefit BBQs with the nonprofits to sell delicious BBQ lunches at New Seasons stores. New Seasons provides the publicity, setup, equipment, food, beverages, and staff to organize and manage the BBQ. The nonprofit partner provides volunteers to help serve and to provide information about its organization, its projects, and important issues. The nonprofits receive 100 percent of the proceeds from the BBQs. New Seasons sets goals each year for the money its benefit BBQ program will raise and shares the results with the community. In 2005, New Seasons' BBQs raised over $40,000, highlighted the work, and facilitated community connections for environmental, human rights, and educational community organizations. At the same time, New Seasons highlighted its values proposition for the beneficiary's members and like-minded community members through media stories, newsletters, and Web sites of its community partners.

As part of achieving its ultimate neighborhood store goal, New Seasons also sets goals for hiring from the local community. It establishes goals for each store and designs its recruiting efforts to utilize community partnerships via outreach through community and neighborhood papers and local job fairs to ensure that the staff has the perspective of the community. Brian Rohter points out, "One of our primary goals is to ensure that our staff in each store reflects the people living in the houses and apartments around the store. At a time when we get four hundred to five hundred applications for every ten jobs, we made the decision to invest in a full-time staff recruiter whose primary job is to make sure our staff represents the diversity of our community."[17] This fosters an authentic connection to the neighborhood and reflects the diversity and culture of the store's customers. For New Seasons, a traditional human resource and business goal has a major impact on its core market-positioning goal.

New Seasons designed its value and value proposition around a core brand position as the ultimate neighborhood market. By establishing priority goals for its community participation and hiring programs, and by measuring its progress against the goals, New Seasons Market drives community impacts that make a difference and create equity for its community-centered brand position.[18] What you measure matters.

Define Your Success

Setting your goals, making them measurable, identifying and tracking the return on investment and the advancement of mission with each marketing strategy, and rewarding and appropriately publicizing the results of your goals can help maximize your marketing impact. You can make your marketing more effective and efficient by harnessing the continuous learning and information provided by measuring results. Integrating traditional marketing goals with your social and environmental goals can actually distinguish and strengthen your marketing efforts and your brand. Defining your own measures of success that integrate all of your bottom lines will reinforce your value and values proposition and create greater alignment with your mission.

Now we're going to focus on your most important relationship—the one with your customers—and how to build long-term connections by clearly addressing their needs, desires, and values.

4

Know your audience

**PRACTICE 4: BE AGGRESSIVELY
CUSTOMER CENTERED**

Today we live in a hypercompetitive world, where standing out requires focus, a unique selling proposition, and a strong commitment to core values. Practice 4 is about being exceptionally focused. Businesses that tend to create sustainable success are aggressively customer centered, focusing on building long-term relationships with their customers.

In the book *Ben & Jerry's Double-Dip*, the trailblazing ice cream visionaries put it this way: "Selling your product is an essential part of any business. It's a means to an end, a way of accomplishing an objective. For a conventional business, the objective is maximizing short-term profitability. For a values-led business, the objective is to build long-term relationships with customers—so we can work together for the greater common social good and make money as well. Building long-term relationships helps both parts of the bottom line. Loyal customer relationships help us to be effective in the community and help us sell our product."[1]

Long-term relationships with customers require you to know your customers, maybe even better than they know themselves.

Take Gabe Luna-Ostaseski, who started MoonDance Painting, the San Francisco Bay Area's first nontoxic, low-odor painting contractor. When Gabe decided to create this business, he knew in his gut lots of customers would prefer an environmentally sensitive painting contractor. Yet very few of these customers would actively search for a company like his because they simply didn't know it existed.

Gabe understood that his company's success was predicated on making sure the eco-friendly customer knew that MoonDance existed. Unfortunately, as with many new businesses, he had only a tiny marketing budget.

Gabe resourcefully contacted the local Whole Foods Market community relations representative and suggested that the store sponsor a "Green Home Series" in which a green designer, builder, landscaper, and painter would come in and make presentations on how people can "green" their homes. The net result was that Gabe was able to connect with the perfect niche of customers who would seek his services—and he did this without spending more than one hundred dollars on marketing.[2]

Noted business author Ron Zemke says the magic in knowing your audience is picking the right customers. He says, "Small businesses don't do a very good job of segmenting. If you've been serving everybody and not thinking about who your core customers are, you're going to be in trouble when business changes."[3] Many companies spend too much time romancing marginal customers at the expense of lavishing more attention on their high-value customers.

This chapter will focus on how you create a deeper relationship with your core customer base. How did Apple or Harley-Davidson create a cult of fiercely loyal customers? Were they just great marketers? No. The reality is they understood the underlying psychology of their customer base, created a product that thrilled the customer, and then developed a brand message that created big word of mouth.

Let's do a quick study of the Hierarchy of Needs theory developed by legendary psychologist Abraham Maslow.[4] We've found this to be a foundational tool for helping us understand our customers. Maslow's defining work in the mid-twentieth century was focused on how human beings aspire to become self-actualized.

Whereas earlier psychologists had primarily studied human neuroses, Maslow focused on fully functioning people to try and understand what motivated them. He created his seminal hierarchy, which premised that people had foundational needs that had to be met (physiological needs like sleep, water, and food). But as these needs were met, people sought higher needs—all the way up to the peak experience of self-actualization.[5]

Maslow's pyramid can actually be applied to any business as well as to any customer. Chip has used this pyramid to help understand what a customer is looking for in a hotel experience.

Maslow's Hierarchy of Needs

At the base of the hotel hierarchy pyramid is a comfortable and clean bed and bathroom. Moving up the pyramid, a quiet room that feels safe and protected is important. The social needs might be addressed by the quality of service the hotel staff provides, and the esteem needs could relate to whether the customer feels treated like a VIP or whether there's any cachet associated with the reputation of the hotel.

Chip believes that the self-actualizing hotel creates a lifelong memory for guests, such that guests feel nurtured, important, and celebrated for who they are as individuals. He calls this "identity refreshment," which will be addressed later in this chapter under "Core Applications." Suffice it to say, you can use this pyramid as a model to better understand what it is your customer is looking for when buying your product or service.

All companies could benefit from asking how their customers might prioritize their own hierarchy of needs. Gabe Luna-Ostaseski may believe that the base need of his customers is a painting contractor who is reliable, affordable, and provides

Hotel Hierarchy of Needs

a paint job that lasts a long time. And their self-actualizing needs may also be met when they feel good about being eco-friendly. Or Gabe may know that some of his customers' base need is for a low-odor paint because of respiratory illness or chemical sensitivities.

In most cases, if you don't satisfy your customers' base needs, it doesn't matter if you get to their self-actualizing needs. But true loyalty—and a long-term relationship—is built at the top of the pyramid. Apple's customers may love its technology (the base need), but its cultish following is fed by the "be different" branding at the top of Apple's hierarchy pyramid. This is what makes Apple devotees feel not only that they are smart rebels of sorts but, more importantly, as if they belong to a community.

As Douglas Atkin, author of *The Culting of Brands,* posits, "The community that surrounds Apple is typical of contemporary neighborhoods. No longer dependent on geographic proximity, they tend to be defined by a state of mind, or collective conviction. Apple brand members (and they definitely see themselves as 'members,' not just buyers) would define themselves by their different attitude to life . . . they have gravitated to a community of people that think more alike, and less like the rest of the world." He goes on to say something rather Maslovian: "The marketing industry has been blind to a need that is so essential it is second only to the compulsion for food and shelter: the desire to belong. To overlook this basic need is to overlook a clear major source of business."[6]

Take a few minutes and imagine a hierarchy of needs for your customer. Create a pyramid and engage a collection of your colleagues in a discussion of your customers' priorities and needs. You might consider sitting down with one of your loyal customers, showing him Maslow's pyramid, and then having him create one that describes his own needs as your customer.

Once you've entered into the mind of your customer, it's time to listen to what's coming out of his mouth. Word of mouth has long been acknowledged as the most effective form of marketing in virtually every industry. Yet today, "word of mouse" is what savvy businesspeople are focused on. Word of mouse is how your company is portrayed in consumer-generated media (CGM) on the Internet. Unlike word of mouth, which tends to be local in nature and can dissipate quickly, word of mouse can circle the globe overnight, last forever on Web sites (leaving a digital trail), and is often found like a signpost along the "highway" that your customer travels when searching the Internet for your product or service.

Pete Blackshaw, chief marketing and client satisfaction officer for Intelliseek (a company that measures and analyzes online "buzz" and word-of-mouth behavior), estimates that over 1.5 billion CGM comments are archived on the Web today, and this is growing by 30 percent annually.[7] The most likely forms of CGM include

- Blogs—First-person narratives that may be about numerous topics but can show up in a search on your company since they index fastest on search engines.
- Message boards and forums—Typically industry- or interest-focused.
- Review or rating sites—Sites like Epinions, TripAdvisor, and Amazon.
- Clubs or groups—These may be user groups that are specific to your product or company, but they are more likely to be related to your industry.
- Direct company feedback—Research shows that nearly 70 percent of consumers who give your company direct feedback (whether online or by calling your headquarters or consumer line) are active across other CGM channels.

- Third-party Web sites—Sites like Complaints.com or My3cents.com.

Whether it's from mouth or mouse, the essential learning here is that you need to create "listening posts" where you can stay close to your customers to understand how they're feeling about you. Gone are the days when you can just rely on traditional consumer surveys that are filled out after your customer has purchased your product or service. Companies that are aggressively customer-centered set up systems that monitor all of the digital and nondigital ways your customer gives feedback to you and the world.

Companies are well served by also considering those Web sites that speak directly to the socially responsible customer, such as Co-op America's National Green Pages, whose database recommends healthy products of all kinds, or 1% for the Planet, an alliance of businesses—started by Patagonia's founder—committed to leveraging their resources to create a healthier planet by donating 1 percent of sales.

Core Applications

Here are four key tools you can use to help your company be more customer-centered:

1. Create an organizing principle for understanding your customer.
2. Engage your customer in creating the product.
3. Understand how your customer feels about the experience.
4. Tap into your listening posts and foster word of mouse.

Create an Organizing Principle for Understanding Your Customer

Maslow's pyramid is one way for you to try to more deeply understand the psychology of your core customer. Joie de Vivre

Hospitality has developed an organizing principle that has helped it create more than thirty extremely unique boutique hotels.

When Chip started the company twenty years ago, he surmised that boutique hotels were sort of like magazines—a niche-oriented, lifestyle-driven product that matched the personality of its core customers. Chip made the decision that each of his hotels would be based upon the personality of a magazine and five adjectives that described the magazine. By using that distinct magazine personality, Chip and his development and design team could articulate a clear vision of how this personality could relate to the guest room design, the type of staff they hired, the unique services and amenities that would be offered, and even the kind of community philanthropy the hotel might pursue.

While this organizing principle helped create an efficient and effective process of creating a compelling product, the real magic was in the identity refreshment it created for its core customer (if you'll recall, identity refreshment was at the top of the hotel pyramid earlier in the chapter). Chip came to realize that customers who fell in love with the hotel viewed it as a kind of aspirational mirror for themselves—the five words used to describe the magazine and the hotel could also apply to those customers, at least on a good day.

For example, Joie de Vivre's first hotel, the Phoenix, is a rock-and-roll hotel in a transitional neighborhood and was designed with *Rolling Stone* magazine in mind, using the words *funky, cool, young-at-heart, adventurous,* and *irreverent.* Of course, most of the Phoenix's guests are young, tattooed musicians from around the world who fit this personality. But there have been many others—like the legendary Dr. Timothy Leary—all raving fans of the Phoenix (who may not fit the demographic of the hotel but certainly fit the personality of those five words).

By staying at the Phoenix, these guests feel funkier, cooler, and more irreverent. Identity refreshment means that this core customer will pay a premium for the experience.

Joie de Vivre has found this magazine approach to be so successful that the company created a cartoon character for its Web site. Yvette, the hotel matchmaker, delivers a five-question personality test to prospective guests. Once a guest has taken the one-minute test, Yvette offers (1) the Joie de Vivre hotels that best fit this guest's personality, (2) profiles of two locals who are similar to this guest along with descriptions of their perfect day at their places of choice, and (3) six unique activities in the area that fit this guest's personality. This mass customization tool creates an emotional link between the company and the prospective guest—so much so that Joie de Vivre books twice as many Web-based hotel reservations (as a percentage of total revenue) than its competitors.

American marketing has historically been based upon customer demographics—what we look like on the outside. But in the past few years, psychographics—what we look like on the inside—have become a far better means of capturing the hearts and minds of customers. Demographics tend to be more tangible and are focused primarily on age, race, or income. Psychographics focus on the more intangible—passions, beliefs, or values. Demographics are often defined by how the world sees us while psychographics are defined more by how we see ourselves.

Demographics are less meaningful today because we don't fit into the somewhat stereotypical boxes we did in the 1950s. Just because a female consumer is forty-two years old and lives in suburban Chicago doesn't necessarily mean she's a housewife with three kids. Finding a way to connect with your customers on a psychographic level is a responsible way of moving beyond the stereotypes that are usually endemic to demographic marketing.

Engage Your Customer in Creating the Product

Most companies create their products in a vacuum, trying to imagine what their customers would appreciate. Wild Planet Toys is one of those smart companies that realizes it will probably meet the needs of its customers better if they are included in the creative process.

Wild Planet is dedicated to developing nonviolent, innovative toys that appeal to both parents and kids. It has experienced nearly a 50 percent compounded annual growth rate for the past few years, not only because of its popular products but also because of its unique approach to being close to its customers. Wild Planet tries to create toys that parents will value and kids will find cool. How does an adult toy creator know what's cool to a kid? Let the kid create the toy.

Danny Grossman, Wild Planet's founder and CEO, came up with the idea for the Kid Inventor Challenge when the company was doing philanthropic work at a low-income housing project. His intention was to teach kids about toy design and involve them in the process as a way of giving back to the community. What surprised Danny was how inventive the kids could be. Nine-year-old Shahid Minapara was shown a glove toy and asked what else he could wear on his hands. Shahid imagined having a light on each finger and then drew a quick design for the Wild Planet team. The design team immediately recognized that it was feasible to produce and had that extra spark of innovation and uniqueness that Wild Planet demands from its toys. Thus, the Kid Inventor Challenge was born.

Today, there are nearly six thousand entries annually, and approximately one hundred winners who join the Kid Inventor Team as toy consultants to the company for one year. As consultants, these kids receive secret sneak peaks at new products and get to keep all of the toys Wild Planet sends them throughout the year. Five kids have even had their ideas made into real toys—receiving royalties from Wild Planet for the life of the products. The company has also created a Toy Opinion Panel as another way for their customers to provide feedback before a new product is launched.

The Kid Inventor Challenge is Wild Planet's way of championing kids—especially those in disadvantaged neighborhoods. It provides children with a positive learning experience, exposes them to a work environment in an engaging way, and makes them feel important. At the same time, Wild Planet creates a relatively inexpensive and unique means of enhancing its research and development efforts. This approach to staying close to the customer also inspires the Wild Planet employees since it's a constant reminder of why there's real meaning in what they do for a living.[8]

Understand How Your Customer Feels about the Experience

When Eric Ryan started his company, method, he was interested in designing household products that were not just effective for cleaning but also aesthetically pleasing—so much so that his customers would prefer to keep method products on the counter as opposed to below the sink. Eric, whose background was branding and marketing, wanted to turn this low-interest consumer category (cleaning products) into something cool. No one had tapped into the "enjoyable" potential of everyday chores, so Eric hired designers to create sexy packaging for dishwashing detergent and liquid hand soap.

As Eric dove further into product development with his partner Adam Lowry, a chemical engineering graduate from Stanford, he came to realize that it would be hard to ask his customers to put their pretty method bottles on the counter—next to food and within a child's reach—when these products could be full of poison. The realization that his soon-to-be competitors produced cleaning products full of nasty chemicals led Eric to his own socially responsible conversion. He quickly turned into a more conscious entrepreneur, committed to producing method products that would be attractive to the eye and nose while also being eco-friendly and safe.

Once Eric and his team launched method in 2001, it became clear to him that he needed to create a means of playing up the cool factor of his brand while also engaging his core customers to see how they felt about the product. Traditional product development might have suggested that he hire cultural anthropologists to observe how his products were being used in the home. And traditional marketing might have suggested billboard advertising near grocery stores. Far from a traditionalist, Eric came up with another solution in concert with Ammo Marketing, his outside marketing agency.

Eric and Ammo erected a temporary "pop-up shop" for method in a vacant storefront in the Union Square shopping area of San Francisco. This unique store concept became a living lab where ambassadors from the company (who weren't primarily focused on sales) could educate customers about the dual benefits of method's modern design and safe ingredients. They created smelling stations where customers could suggest their favorite scents for products. Word of mouth and free editorial print media about this odd little shop spread fast, and eventually the likes of Robin Williams were dropping in. Conversion rates of customers were 80 percent, and the average purchase was twenty dollars—pretty good for a shop exclusively focused on basic household cleaning products. Furthermore, method hosted targeted influencer events, including a Thursday happy hour for business professionals, and catered parties for specific target groups like *Dwell* magazine subscribers, Volvo drivers, local philanthropists, and the corporate staff of Design Within Reach.

The shop was scheduled to be open for just two months, but by midfall it was clear this guerrilla marketing initiative was a success, so the shop remained open through the Christmas holidays. For approximately the same price as a traditional billboard, the pop-up shop created a brand shrine for this new company. The customer could touch and feel its unique home products, and the method team could evaluate customers' reactions to the various lines of products. This was clearly better than the typical focus group behind a one-way mirror/window.

While this is a good example of how to connect intimately with your customers, it also shows how companies can lead by example. Eric Ryan didn't originally enter this business to be socially responsible, but in his research of the industry and in his early product development phase, he quickly realized he could make his product more eco-friendly and still serve the customer base he was seeking. In method's case, its success has influenced its more established competition to start "cleaning up" household cleaning products so that the whole product category is becoming more environmentally sensitive.[9]

Tap into Your Listening Posts and Foster Word of Mouse

Ray Anderson is a captain of industry who also experienced a conversion. As founder and CEO of Interface, Inc., one of the largest carpet manufacturers in the world (with twenty-six factories on four continents), Ray's company is in one of the most environmentally unsustainable industries in the world.

But in the mid-1990s, Ray made a decision that would change the course of his company. On discovering Paul Hawken's revolutionary *The Ecology of Commerce* he has said, "I read it, and it changed my life . . . it was an epiphany. I wasn't halfway through it before the vision I sought became clear, along with a powerful sense of urgency to do something."[10] Ray decided

Interface would become "the first fully sustainable industrial enterprise, anywhere."[11] The company would no longer use virgin nylon yard to stitch its fabrics, its offices and factories would create renewable power sources, and it would have a goal of no waste by reclaiming its own products and using them as raw materials for new textiles. You can read Ray's remarkable story in his book, *Mid-Course Correction.*

In the midst of this environmental revolution in the company, Ray and his management team also decided they needed to get closer to their suppliers and customers. Interface worked with its suppliers by insisting the products it bought be recyclable and nontoxic. And the company started sending this new message to its customers by helping them think differently about carpeting—to imagine the idea of renting rather than buying carpeting or to imagine the idea of carpeting in squares as opposed to full sheets of carpet (this had been done in the commercial sector for years but had never been available to the general retail market).

Interface's FLOR product sprang out of this staying close to the customer. Similar to method, the impetus behind FLOR was initially aesthetic: to give customers the ability to be a little more creative with their choice of carpet. Since FLOR is a modular carpet tile system, it allows consumers to customize a pattern for the home or office. From a sustainability perspective, FLOR tiles use a lighter adhesive and allow customers to replace one square at a time. The customer sends the square back and FLOR recycles it. People no longer have to replace an entire room of carpet because of one stain that won't go away. So sustainability can mean affordability.

While Ray's revolution might not be televised, it certainly found an appropriate home on the Web. The Web was the perfect medium for Interface to get its sustainable message out far and wide. More specifically, the Interface management team could use its Web site as a listening post for its new FLOR product. Go to the company's Web site and you'll see an inspiring blend of marketing the product and messaging the sustainable mission. On the site, the company has taken a sophisticated approach to engaging customers in education and dialogue about FLOR. Whether it's a discussion with a designer about how to use the product, customer designs and testimonials, or specifics on the socially responsible elements of its product, Interface has effectively reinvented the consumer carpet category. And with the "FLOR boards" blog, it has instituted a sort of democratization of design—with everyone from professional designers to DIY weekend warriors evangelizing about the "fun" of carpet installation and design.

Chip DeGrace, vice president of marketing for Interface-FLOR, says, "The FLOR boards community has developed a new design vocabulary . . . the site helps us to not only take the pulse of our customer, but fosters ideas that are instrumental in new product development."[12]

NEW SEASONS MARKET

KNOW YOUR CUSTOMER

New Seasons Market sees engagement with its customers as an ongoing dialogue that creates strong relationships. The owners of New Seasons looked at what they had learned from customers over years in the grocery and natural foods industries. Two key lessons were that customers wanted shopping to be easy and fun and that customers want to be treated as individuals. As we discussed in chapter 1, New Seasons had designed the mix of its product offerings based upon understanding its customers' needs for natural foods and conventional products. New Seasons also used its knowledge of its customers to design the shopping experience. New Seasons asked, "What are the things that *don't* make shopping fun and easy?" What it came up with was a list of the many little annoyances typical to grocery shopping that stood in the way. From this list of the most typical shoppers' complaints—and requests—New Seasons created a set of policies that it calls "The Fine Print." New Seasons made a pledge to its customers, posted it in every store and printed it on every grocery bag and on its Web site. The pledge states:

"Open the Next Register" Policy
More than 2 people in line?
We'll open another check stand right away.

"Staffing" Policy
We hire people who really mean it when they say, "Have a nice day." We treat them as well as we want them to treat you.

"Helping You Find it" Policy
We'll escort you to the spot (unless you just want directions).

"Product Returns" Policy
If it's not exactly what you want, or if you don't like it for any reason, bring it back for a no hassle return. We'll replace it or refund your money with a smile. We promise.

"Eating in the Store" Policy
Go for it. Please pay for it on the way out.

"Discount" Policy
Enjoy a senior discount every Wednesday—
10 percent off almost everything for those 65 or better.

"You Break It" Policy
If you break it . . . don't worry. Accidents happen.

"Problems" Policy
We have, find and make solutions.
Visit the Solutions Counter at the front of the store.

"Special Request" Policy
"Yes."

"Squeaky Wheel" Policy
Our shopping carts will be oiled and maintained so they don't
drag, squeak, or otherwise annoy you.

New Seasons walks the talk of The Fine Print every day. It
also has established listening posts to continually learn
about and be responsive to its customers. The Solutions
Counter (mentioned above in the Problems Policy) is located
at the front of every store and is staffed by someone whose
main job is to answer customer questions, solve problems,
and otherwise listen to customers. New Seasons provides
suggestion cards, responds directly to the customer who sub-
mitted the suggestion, and posts the cards in the store with
New Seasons' answers or solutions written right on them.
Often, suggestions from customers result in immediate action. A customer card expressed that the many labels on eggs
(cage-free, ova-free, grain-fed, etc.) are confusing. New Seasons developed a glossary that explains each term and
posted it on the egg case in every store. The bulletin board at
the front of each store is full of cards from customers and solutions from New Seasons. "There are no layers between us
and the customer," explains Brian Rohter. "People are blown
away when we respond, and we learn a lot by reading and listening to what customers are saying."[13] By listening to,
learning from, and visibly acting upon customers' suggestions, New Seasons Market meets shoppers' needs and desires, builds a relationship of trust, and lives up to its promise
of being a place where it's easy and fun to shop.[14]

Know Your Audience

To be truly customer centered is to place your customers' needs and desires at the top of your business goals (your own hierarchy of needs pyramid). If you meet these goals, you will find yourself well on your way to building the lasting relationships that can transform a run-of-the-mill venture into a successful— and socially responsible—business.

Now we're going to ask you to step outside of your comfort zone and question conventional wisdom while you expand your customer base and your vision for your business.

Question conventional wisdom

PRACTICE 5: DON'T LIMIT YOUR MARKET

Are you satisfied with the status quo? Has your business maxed out with respect to growth? We doubt it. Imagine your business ten years from now and four times larger than it is today. Where will all those new customers come from? If you're concerned that growth means you'll have to turn your back on being socially responsible—don't worry. The two are not mutually exclusive. In this chapter we'll show you why.

The reality is that most businesses underestimate the size of the market for their product or service. If you do this, you're in good company. John Mackey, founder and CEO of Whole Foods Market, estimated that just one hundred appropriate store locations existed in the United States for Whole Foods when the company went public in 1992 (at the time, it had twelve stores). Now it's closing in on two hundred stores.[1] Clearly, he underestimated the market for organic and natural foods. And thus far, Whole Foods's track record proves that such growth can be achieved while remaining true to one's core values and socially responsible roots.

It isn't just well-known socially responsible companies that underestimate their markets. In this book we at times refer to large, profitable, and sometimes controversial companies that provide relevant examples, if not a clear socially responsible mission. The truth is, whether traditional or progressive, profitable organizations have some common ground. We suggest that you can learn from both.

In 1960, Sam Walton was quoted in a magazine article as saying that his young company, Wal-Mart, had grown about as big as it could get with its nine stores. The condition that limited his perceived growth potential was his ability to visit all of his stores within a day. You know the rest of the story, as that behemoth now reports the highest sales of any company in the world ($285 billion in 2004).[2]

A natural tendency is to focus your business plan and marketing on who and what you know. In many ways, businesses have a tendency to market to themselves—a market of one. And if you're entering an established market with competitors who've been operating for quite some time, you may assume that they've done their homework and maximized their market reach. Question those assumptions.

It may be that the market leader is focusing only on the primary market—-the customers who most obviously would buy the product or service. Yet the secondary market may be untapped and, who knows, it might be even bigger than the primary market.

Think of Southwest Airlines, a Texas-based air carrier that also underestimated its potential market back in the late 1970s. At that time, when most other airlines were rushing to grow due to airline deregulation, CEO Herb Kelleher proclaimed that Southwest Airlines was going to be just an intrastate airline within Texas. Yet Southwest's compelling value proposition of giving middle and lower income Americans the "freedom" (the company's mantra and tagline) to experience air travel inexpensively opened up a secondary market. And this secondary market of travelers who previously would have taken a bus, driven, or not traveled at all, has helped to dramatically grow the American airline industry.[3] Southwest questioned the conventional wisdom that air travel has to be expensive and bland (not a particularly compelling combination).

Whether you're in a start-up or a large company, you are well served by questioning your assumptions. Here's a series of questions you and your senior leadership should consider as you imagine your company's growth:

- What market segments are currently underserved in your marketplace, and why are they underserved? Is it based upon some faulty assumptions?
- What core assumptions are you using to define your markets? Have you unconsciously limited your market based upon those assumptions?
- What is your biggest fear in going after new market segments? Do you fear that it will conflict with your existing base of customers? While it's wise to consider potential risks, perhaps you just need a better sense of the buying patterns and attitudes of that secondary market.
- Without intention, are you excluding customers based upon ethnicity, race, gender, sexual orientation, class, age, education level, or location? Are changing demographics making this an even more serious long-term problem if you don't open up to a broader market?
- Are there social, environmental, and/or business benefits (known as the triple bottom line) in serving markets others ignore? By reaching out to these new customer segments, are you increasing the market for your business and for your competitors? (A win-win approach to success—prosperity for all.)

We're going to go out on a limb here and say this: most so-cially responsible businesses limit their marketing scope just to the true believers. These already faithful patrons are the "low hanging fruit"—the most obvious market for your product or service. Yet by limiting your scope, you are potentially placing a glass ceiling on your expansion. Or by tailoring your market-ing just to the true believers, you may be missing out on other audiences. For example, with the growth of socially responsible companies in the mainstream, socially responsible investment companies are realizing that they need to broaden their adver-tising to a larger audience beyond just those who may read po-litically progressive magazines like the *Utne* magazine.

Core Applications

We recommend four steps that you should follow in evaluating whether you and your team have been expansive enough in your thinking:

1. Evaluate your assumptions about your market.
2. Reposition your product so that it reaches a larger market.
3. Develop your marketing materials so that they speak to untapped markets.
4. Hire staff and create strategic partnerships that reflect your commitment to serving a larger marketplace.

Evaluate Your Assumptions about Your Market

Whether you're part of a big company that has neglected poorer parts of the world or you're a small local company that has un-consciously imagined that your market was limited to your neighborhood, question every assumption that drives your business. Reconsider your price point, your packaging size, or your delivery model. A market may be right under your nose that you haven't considered.

Professors C. K. Prahalad and Stuart L. Hart have studied how multinational corporations tend to misjudge the potential market size in developing countries. They believe the six core mistaken assumptions that are relevant, both to big and small companies, when it comes to evaluating the large lower-income segment of the market include

1. The poor are not our target customers because with our current cost structures, we cannot profitably compete for that market.
2. The poor cannot afford and have no use for the products and services sold in developed markets.
3. Only developed markets appreciate and will pay for new technology. The poor can use the previous generation of technology.
4. The bottom of the pyramid (economically) is not important to the long-term viability of our business—we can leave that to governments and nonprofits.
5. Managers are not excited by business challenges that have a humanitarian dimension.
6. Intellectual excitement is in the developed markets.

Each of these assumptions obscures the value of a huge percentage of the population. Four billion of the world's six billion people live in developing countries. If the incomes of the world's poor (defined as less than $2 per day) were increased by $1 per day, this would account for over $1 trillion in world economic growth per year. Sometimes it just requires a few role models to debunk faulty assumptions.[4]

In India, for instance, Arvind Mills, the world's fifth largest denim manufacturer, has introduced an entirely new delivery system for blue jeans. Of course, the vast majority of Indians couldn't afford jeans at $40 to $60 per pair. So Arvind questioned the assumption about how jeans were to be delivered to the customer and introduced Ruf & Tuf jeans, a ready-to-make kit of jeans components (denim, zipper, rivets, and a patch) priced at $6. Kits were distributed through thousands of local tailors in small villages whose self-interest motivated them to market the kits to the community. Ruf & Tuf jeans are now the largest selling jeans in India.[5]

Hewlett-Packard has a history of questioning assumptions and making a difference, which is summed up in its "HP for the World" slogan. Hewlett-Packard chose to challenge the mistaken assumptions that Prahalad and Hart cited when it created its "world e-inclusion" campaign, dedicated to providing technology, products, and services that meet the needs of the world's poor while enhancing HP's business opportunities in emerging markets that its competition hadn't seriously considered.

For example, in Costa Rica, Hewlett-Packard questioned the assumption that rural villages were not a market for technology because the villagers couldn't individually afford the equipment. In partnership with MIT Media Lab and the Costa Rica Foundation for Sustainable Development, HP developed digital "telecenters" for the town center of villages, with high-speed Internet connections and a number of other technology products that villagers could use communally for a price. And, of course, HP now has a leg up on the competition in terms of building a relationship with these villagers as their incomes grow and they can afford technology in their homes.[6]

Evaluating your assumptions about your market is just as relevant to small companies as it is to multinationals. You might operate a small chain of regional electronics stores and have never thought of advertising to the Spanish-language market. While Hispanic individuals tend to make less than Caucasians in America, statistics show that Hispanic families are more likely to live in multigenerational households.[7] This can mean a high household income due to multiple wage earners under one roof, which means that your advertising may even be more fruitful to this market.

Reposition Your Product So That It Reaches a Larger Market

Vegan restaurants have a reputation (deserved or not) for being spartan, styleless, and only appropriate for righteous people who refuse to eat animal products—usually those who do it more for political or environmental reasons than anything else. Twelve years ago, Chip was involved in starting a restaurant in San Francisco called Millennium, which questioned all these reputational assumptions.

Millennium aspired to make vegan cuisine sexy, abundant, and appealing to the masses. Chip realized that Millennium's potential market size could be much larger if it reached out to a customer base beyond vegans and vegetarians. He and his partners asked the kinds of questions that were listed earlier in the chapter, but they also realized that they needed to consult with a wider audience.

Chip invited a diverse group of thirty friends and business associates (only one of whom was a vegetarian) to have a complimentary dinner at Millennium soon after it opened. At the dinner, the chef and Chip's partner talked about the value of a vegan diet and invited the group to try a number of unique dishes. But most importantly, Chip welcomed the group to talk about what kind of people might be interested in this "good for yourself, good for the planet" diet. Then the group was provided with education, tips, and recipes that could help them "go vegan" for one month until they came back thirty days later to have a follow-up dinner and discussion.

While only half of the group made it back for the dinner, they were very engaged. Their brainstorming led to a number of insightful ideas for new markets that Millennium could tap: cardiologists and other doctors who advise cigar-chomping business execs to modify their diet, fitness trainers who advise their clients to seek out a low-fat diet, religious or ethnic groups who follow a meatless diet. More than a dozen market segments were identified with action plans of how to reach out to each. Based upon the high volume and diversity of diners at Millennium, compared to the normal vegan restaurant, it's pretty clear that this outreach was successful.

The best idea that arose was to create a monthly event to emphasize how vegan cuisine can help you feel sexier and more clever. Since many aphrodisiacs are herbal, the group came up with the idea of having a Full Moon Aphrodisiac Night once per month. On the night of a full moon, couples could enjoy a fixed-price three-course vegan feast intended to arouse an amorous mood, and then—because Millennium was located in a boutique hotel—those couples choosing this package would receive a free night upstairs (which cost the restaurant very little since the hotel and restaurant were managed by the same company, Joie de Vivre Hospitality).

You can imagine that the Full Moon Aphrodisiac Night had lots of press potential. More than one hundred articles have been written about this package, and it regularly sells out at Millennium. Most importantly, it helped position this vegan restaurant as something other than a funky, humorless place to grab a healthy meal. And Millennium now has one of the most diverse customer bases of any restaurant in San Francisco with its tattooed animal activists with shaved heads sitting next to starched investment bankers in suspenders.

Millennium actively sought out new markets of customers, but sometimes companies just stumble upon these opportunities. Dole started producing organic bananas for fast-growing Whole Foods Markets only to find out that half the demand for its organic bananas comes from conventional supermarkets. Organic Valley cooperative, a large national supplier of organic milk, similarly grew fast to help support Whole Foods' demand but now finds that its largest customer is Publix, an upscale regional supermarket chain in the Southeast that is significantly larger than Whole Foods.[8]

Start your process by reviewing any data you have on who your existing core market might be and whether that provides you enough room to grow your business. Use the questions on page 79 to establish a ritual for how you question your assumptions. Consider bringing in outsiders to help you open your mind to larger markets you hadn't even considered.

Develop Your Marketing Materials So That They Speak to Untapped Markets

Fortunately, in the past ten years we've seen a dramatic shift in the marketing materials of most companies, such that there's much more diversity in the casting of their ads. It's only logical for companies to cast their ads and target their media to the diverse markets that they serve. Yet many organizations are reluctant to go much beyond a gratuitous small photo depicting multi-ethnic subjects in a marketing brochure.

Kimpton Hotels and Restaurants is the largest boutique hotelier in America, with more than forty hotels in over twenty metropolitan markets. While it owns a large percentage of its hotels, it also acts as a third-party manager for hotel owners who are looking for a competent hotel management company and brand. Because Kimpton has so many interested constituencies—from its investors to the owners who hire it to a mainstream clientele of customers—it would be understandable if it were to be slightly conservative in its approach to addressing the gay, lesbian, bisexual, and transgender (GLBT) market. The truth is all of the other major national chains have been very reluctant to publicly engage this market for conventional reasons—the perceived notion that they would risk alienating their core market.

Kimpton was built upon its core values of diversity and fairness. Based in San Francisco, the company has long been at the forefront of progressive hiring practices within the GLBT community. And for years, Kimpton had targeted some of its marketing to this community. Yet it was mostly undercover, attending gay travel trade shows, marketing to gay travel agents—nothing that was promoted to the community at large. But around the time San Francisco Mayor Gavin Newsom made the controversial decree that GLBT marriages would be performed in San Francisco (Valentine's Day 2004), Kimpton decided to finally "out" itself as a gay-friendly company.

Andrew Freeman, former vice president of public relations and strategic partnerships, explains that Kimpton has always been a gay-friendly company. In terms of marketing, he says, "We were clear that the GLBT market appreciated our hotels given our lifestyle-driven product that is both stylish and fun. We also knew that the GLBT market has high-disposable income and spends a larger percentage of its money on travel than the average American. Yet, as a national company, we knew there were some substantial risks in publicly promoting ourselves as 'gay-friendly' beyond locations like San Francisco, New York and L.A."[9]

Freeman continues, "Initially once the Mayor made his decree, we launched a San Francisco 'Honeymoon Package,' which was only promoted by press release. The response from the media was huge and we booked an enormous amount of business. That gave us confidence to take it to the next step."[10]

The next step was hiring a company that was an expert in GLBT marketing in order to produce a comprehensive national campaign. This company—Witick Combs Communications—helped create a June Pride Package that Kimpton rolled out nationally but still in a very targeted way.

It wasn't until the fall of 2004 that the risks of this campaign became evident. Kimpton launched an ad campaign with the tagline "Our Properties Are as Unique as You Are" with the image of an attractive African-American gay man holding a puppy in his lap. It followed this with a relaunch of its Web site that included a new section exclusively devoted to GLBT travelers that was both sexy and welcoming.

A "family values" group took notice and decided to target Kimpton with a shame campaign. The group sent out anti-Kimpton press releases and spent two days jamming Kimpton's phone lines and e-mail with dissent. Freeman says those two days were pretty scary, but senior leadership at Kimpton (which is heterosexual) never wavered from its commitment to this marketing campaign to the GLBT community. After a couple of days, things got back to normal and Kimpton now cites the fact that 20-30 percent of its recent growth in year-over-year revenues is coming from the GLBT market.[11] Its Web site is truly a model for how a company can reach out to an untapped market. You'll find a specific section for rave reviews from GLBT travelers about why they love Kimpton Hotels, along with Kimpton's unique approach to working with its GLBT employees, the GLBT community, and its Red Ribbon campaign that raises money for the National AIDS Fund.[12]

The GLBT market has $500 billion of buying power in America.[13] It's one of many niche segments that most companies overlook. But just featuring an ethnic, senior, or GLBT face in your brochure isn't enough these days; you've got to understand your target market and appeal to its needs in an authentic way.

While inherent risks are associated with taking a stand, running a socially responsible enterprise requires that leadership stay true to its organization's mission and values. This may at times include marketing that might be perceived as risky.

Having faced their own share of controversy, ice cream entrepreneurs Ben and Jerry viewed taking risks in a very pragmatic way when they were running their company, "It's controversial for a business to take stands that aren't in its own self-interest, because that's not the norm. We've learned that some people are going to be tremendously impressed by our positions and buy more ice cream. A very small number of people are going to be tremendously impressed and buy less. Some people will be completely unaffected. Anything that's not pabulum is going to alienate some people. And that goes for traditional marketing as well."[14]

In Kimpton's case, marketing to the GLBT community served its self-interests and made a difference.

Hire Staff and Create Strategic Partnerships That Reflect Your Commitment to Serving a Larger Marketplace

ShoreBank was established with the primary focus of providing access to credit for minority entrepreneurs. It has been a model organization in many ways, including diversity at all levels of management. From senior corporate leadership to the management of branches, ShoreBank built a team that reflects the community.

Since the church is such an important crossroads for the African American community, ShoreBank created its Faith-Based Banking^{SM} program with customized financial services to churches and their congregations.

ShoreBank realized that providing financial services to churches could assure strong vital institutions, help spark community development and job creation through housing and development programs, and encourage savings, home ownership, and business development among parishioners. Dr. Clyde White, a banker at ShoreBank and a minister, recognized the potential in this market in the mid-1990s. To build the Faith-Based Banking[SM] program, he hired bankers who understood the culture and needs of churches. As he has grown the program, Dr. White has continued to hire bankers who hold divinity degrees and serve as ministers. The Faith-Based Banking[SM] program now banks over six hundred churches and is seen as a national model.[15]

One cautionary note to sum up this chapter: be careful not to lose your commitment to social responsibility as you expand to a larger market. Automaker Toyota has a hit on its hands with the hybrid Prius that initially wowed the environmental community and then became more of a crossover hit with the mainstream as gas prices climbed. Still, Toyota decided that to attract a larger market, it needed to create a more stylish alternative. Thus, its Lexus SUV was repositioned into a hybrid model, offering fuel efficiency and luxury at the same time.

However, early test results reveal that the SUV hybrid could be a wolf in sheep's clothing as the real product offering is a larger engine with no additional fuel economy. The *New York Times* reported on the Lexus hybrid's poor fuel consumption, lamenting, "Toyota's motivation in pushing hybrid technology may turn out to be a different shade of green than we've been led to believe, one much closer to the color of money."[16] This may be an example of marketing that maddens (your core customer), not marketing that matters.

QUESTION CONVENTIONAL WISDOM

For years, an increasing number of grocery stores have been closing in urban neighborhoods. Most grocery chains and mid- to high-end retailers do not open locations in inner cities; therefore many neighborhoods are left underserved and without easy access to healthy food. As New Seasons began adding stores in Portland, conventional wisdom would have identified numerous affluent areas of the city and its suburbs for store locations. But New Seasons noticed that the mixed-income Concordia neighborhood lacked a major grocery store and that residents of the area had few options to find organic, local, and specialty foods. Rather than relying on exclusionary formulas like the percentage of high-income households, New Seasons relied on the core premise of its business that everyone wants access to healthy and delicious food. It recognized an opportunity in a neighborhood where community leaders had protested the closing of stores and where the neighborhood association had appealed to the city about the need for stores and services.

New Seasons engaged the area's neighborhood associations, community-based organizations, schools, churches, and existing area businesses to determine the community's needs. As the store was built, New Seasons partnered with the same organizations to recruit managers and staff that would reflect the rich ethnic and cultural diversity of the community. The day the Concordia store opened felt more like a community festival than a retail opening. The store has exceeded its sales projections, is one of the busiest in the New Seasons family, and is seen as a community hub by neighbors.

In 2005, New Seasons opened another store in urban North Portland. The Arbor Lodge store was built on the site where a national chain supermarket had been closed for over two decades, with the building being used as a warehouse for armored cars. During the years that these stores were being developed, New Seasons' leadership served on the regional government's food policy committee and helped develop recommendations that would encourage other grocers to locate in low-income areas.

New Seasons' CEO Brian Rohter is clear about his reasons for questioning conventional wisdom. "I think there is a certain latent racism that drives a lot of decision-makers in this country. I don't understand why the desire to eat healthy, good food and to be treated in a respectful way would be limited to upper-middle-class white people. And we have proven that all kinds of people, regardless of race or where they are on the economic spectrum, share the same desire to feed their families fresh, healthy food and to get service with a smile."[17]

Questioning conventional wisdom has built two of the company's most successful stores and has created over three hundred jobs in an economically challenged area. It has also helped bust the myth that perpetuates a lack of many services in inner city neighborhoods. It has demonstrated that the disparity of services may not be based on a rational economic or business model but is perhaps due to not testing assumptions that limit a business's customer base—ultimately redlining entire communities from access to services and the economic base that business investment brings.[18]

Don't Limit Your Market

We've shown how questioning conventional wisdom and expanding your vision can open up opportunities you hadn't imagined. Remember that questioning assumptions about who is the customer, designing your product or service to respond to broader needs, creating marketing that reflects and resonates with your larger audience, and building connections to your broader customer base through your hiring, supply, and partnership decisions can all enhance the economic and social performance of your company.

Now let's take a look at the power of communication when you share both your value and your values with your customer.

What's driving the customer decision?

PRACTICE 6: COMMUNICATE VALUE AND VALUES

Socially responsible companies must strike a healthy balance between the value proposition they offer to their customers and the social values they express in the creation of their product and in their marketing. A value proposition is a clear statement of the tangible results a customer gets from using your products or services. The socially responsible message has come to be known as the values proposition, as it allows a company to express its core values in order to clearly differentiate itself from the competition. Most importantly, this differentiator also provides customers with an opportunity to express their own values.

Unfortunately, some socially responsible start-ups make the mistake of operating as if their value proposition is far less important than their values proposition. While that may be true for some of their customers, the reality is that many of those companies never make it to their second year. They've forgotten a basic rule for running a profitable business: your product or service must be competitive in the marketplace.

Michael Crooke, former president and CEO of Patagonia, says, "It doesn't matter if you're eco-groovy, (your product) still has to look right, fit right, be the right color and be high quality. Fifteen years ago, we thought if it was hemp, it was okay to be frumpy; that's not okay anymore—you're frumpy, you're bankrupt."[1]

The good news is there is evidence that companies can strike a healthy balance between value proposition and values without too much compromise. Business professors from the University of Michigan and Harvard found that three-quarters of the ninety-five empirical studies they surveyed established a neutral or positive correlation between social or environmental performance and financial performance.[2] In other words, it is possible to do well financially and to do some good in the world. In fact, there may be a symbiotic relationship between the two.

What are the risks of being out of balance between value and values? Wal-Mart is perhaps the prime example of a company that has been too value focused (lower prices at any cost) without a clear statement of values—internally and externally. Until recently, and undoubtedly due to media pressure, Wal-Mart had a real blind spot regarding its values proposition. Web sites like Wal-Mart Watch and the film *Wal-Mart: The High Cost of Low Price* were produced by customer activists to educate the public about the company's negative impact locally and globally.

The negative press has been so damaging that Wal-Mart has begun to consistently miss its Wall Street estimates of quarterly revenues and net income, leading to a dramatic weakening in Wal-Mart's stock value. Remarkably, the largest company in the world (in terms of revenue) now trades at a discount on the stock exchange, compared to peers like Target, partially due to the company's reputation being tarnished because of a perceived lack of values in its operations and a missing values-driven message in its marketing. As Patrick McKeever, a stock analyst, suggests, "This stock is subject to considerable headline risk,"[3] referring to the almost weekly bouts of bad news surrounding Wal-Mart's community and worker relations.

On the other side of the fence is the Body Shop—once the flagship business model of the socially responsible community. Founder Anita Roddick brilliantly marketed her bath and body products company as being values-driven in its practices. But over time, the actual product quality began to suffer. Serious questions started to arise about the "goodness" of the ingredients and the veracity of some of the Body Shop's responsible trade claims. With new competitors in the marketplace, the Body Shop's overreliance on its values claims and its underreliance on improving the value of its product has led to a large drop in profits and a sizable shrinking of the number of stores around the world.[4] In essence, the Body Shop took its eye off of the value proposition.

Customers' decisions are driven by their perception of your reputation—both in delivering a great product and in doing it in a responsible fashion. Edelman PR Worldwide commissioned a study that found that corporate reputation was the second most important driver of customer demand only after the perception of the quality of a company's products or services.[5]

How do you determine the healthy balance of value and values for your company in product development and in marketing to your customer? You need to consider the key ways that your company can deliver and market its value proposition. In the book *The Myth of Excellence,* authors Ryan Mathews and Fred Crawford suggest that five attributes define the competitive playing field: product, price, access, service, and experience.[6]

One question for each of the five attributes can help you clarify your value proposition to customers relative to your competition:

- Product—What's the quality perception of your product versus your competition's?
- Price—How are you priced compared to your competition?
- Access—How easy are you to find and use?
- Service—How do your customers feel about you as a result of doing business with you?
- Experience—How do your customers feel about themselves as a result of doing business with you?

Mathews and Crawford suggest that most successful companies realize they can't dominate across the board on all five attributes, so they instead find one or two in which they can dominate while making sure they aren't seriously inferior on any of the others. Ask yourself, "How does my product or service measure up on these five attributes compared to my competitors?"

IBM Business Consulting Services produced a similar study titled "Deeper Customer Insight."[7] While IBM agreed with the Mathews-Crawford premise that there are various attributes you can compete upon, it suggested that the key determinant of your success is how well you understand which attributes are most important to your particular customer.

For example, it found two primary kinds of grocery shoppers—those who do a weekly or monthly stockpiling of grocery items (replenishment) and those who do a quick replacement of a few key items (convenience). What's important to replenishment shoppers is that products are reliably in stock and they can get all their shopping done in one place. Convenience shoppers are more focused on speed and ease of shopping. IBM found that on average, 58 percent of shoppers were heavily focused on replenishment while 23 percent were more convenience driven, but for certain stores these percentages could be wildly different. The success of a particular store was significantly determined by how well the store acknowledged whether its customers were primarily replenishment or convenience driven and then how well the store provided the attributes to satisfy the needs of that particular kind of customer.[8]

Now that we've defined the value proposition, let's turn our attention for a moment to how companies focus on values with their customers. There are many types of values propositions: environmentally sustainable manufacturing or sourcing, the part your company plays in the community, how you invest a portion of your revenues or profits in philanthropic activities. Thankfully, the list is endless. The most important question for you to ask yourself is, "What makes this product socially responsible?" If you have a hard time answering that question, then you shouldn't even consider trying to trumpet the values proposition to your customers as it will confuse them.

How can you identify the elements that influence your customer's perception of your value and values proposition? If you recall, back in chapter 4 we introduced how you could use Maslow's Hierarchy of Needs to chart out what your customer may be seeking. Each customer has a different set of motivators that impact how he or she makes product decisions. For some, a base need may be getting a good product at a fair price, while the base need for others may be the assurance that they are buying from a company they perceive to be socially responsible. If you haven't already created a pyramid, we suggest you do it now.

How can you understand the pyramid that's appropriate for your customers and how they use value versus values when deciding what to buy? Here are three basic rules that will help you:

- Define your core customers. Let's call the typical core customer the bull's-eye because she is your perfect target. Consider giving the bull's-eye a name and a full identity. What kind of car does she drive? What does she do with her free time? What social causes does she support? Once you have a clear picture in your head of this customer, ask what's at the base of her pyramid. In other words, why is she buying this product in the first place? We've found it helpful to ask that same question over and over and over again. With each asking of the question, you may get a deeper understanding of what the core drivers are in leading customers to buy this product. When in doubt, you might consider creating focus groups so that you can put these questions directly to your bull's-eye customers.

- Determine what percentage of your total revenue currently comes from those core customers. You can learn this through empirical data (for example, if you have a loyalty club of regular customers, what percentage of your total revenue comes from them?). Or you can learn this by interviewing your line staff who come into contact regularly with your customers—they probably have a good understanding of how many of your customers are bull's-eyes. The higher the percentage of bull's-eyes, the more you can rely on what you learned from the rule above. The lower the percentage, the more you have to apply that same practice of creating a pyramid to your secondary customer niches. One way of plotting this graphically is to imagine a dartboard. The bigger the bull's-eye, the less space you will allocate to your secondary customers.

- The larger the market, the larger the dartboard and the more likely that the bull's-eye is a smaller percentage of the whole dartboard. Many socially responsible companies find that their bull's-eye customers are heavily influenced by the values message, but that their casual customers are less so. As you move from being a tiny underdog brand into being one of the leaders in your product category, you may find that you have to alter your marketing message to be more value driven since the percentage of your customers who are outside the bull's-eye will grow. Conversely, the more generic your product, the more likely you are in a commoditized product category, which opens up the potential for you to distinguish your product by being the values-driven offering in the marketplace. When your competitors have very little differentiation based upon product, price, or access, it opens up the possibility that the values proposition can be your way of reaching out to a bigger audience. Working Assets did this with phone service; New Leaf Paper did it with paper products; Clif Bar did it with energy bars.

Core Applications

We recommend four steps that you should follow to assure that you have the right mix of value and values in your marketing message:

1. Don't lose sight of your customers' core decision-making drivers.
2. Reach out to the core values of your bull's-eye customers.
3. As you grow, recognize that your message needs to resonate with a wider audience.
4. If you're purchased, influence your parent company.

Don't Lose Sight of Your Customers' Core Decision-Making Drivers

Quite often, socially responsible businesses offer their customers multiple benefits. The question is, which benefits, those that are value driven or values driven, have the greatest influence in helping your customer choose your product?

Kim and Jason Graham-Nye discovered an environmentally friendly, convenient, and highly absorbent diaper option in Australia in 2002. They fell in love with the product and bought the rights to market it in the United States, launching gDiapers in 2005. The value proposition is summarized on their Web site: "Imagine taking your baby's soiled diaper and simply flushing it down the toilet. No more smell. No more diaper. No more diaper pail. You're putting waste right where it belongs, in the toilet. Not in a landfill."[9]

What we have here is a product that expands the customer offering beyond just cloth or disposable. Both of these historical options have advantages and disadvantages. Cloth is the more sustainable option (since 50 million disposable diapers end up in American landfills every day) but can be both a hassle and an energy drain, depending on laundering methods. Disposables are dominant (95 percent of the market) because they are convenient for parents. But they are not convenient for the planet.

gDiapers incorporate a two-part system. The flushable inner refill fits into a pair of colorful "little g" pants. When the flushable part becomes soiled, it can simply be flushed down the toilet. So gDiapers have the advantage of being sustainably driven but are more convenient than cloth.

How would you market this new product to the American customer? You could promote the positive impact on the planet. You could promote the fact that gDiapers does not contain the cup of oil used in a regular disposable diaper. You could promote the comfort for babies. You could promote the functionality and convenience to the parent. You could promote the fashion of the colorful "little g" pants. If you try to promote all of those equally, the customer may get confused, so you have to make some choices.

If you go to its Web site, you'll see how gDiapers has crafted its message based upon its perception of its customers' needs pyramid. You'll see a genuine "voice" on the site (including the fact that the founders of gDiapers mention they have two kids) that is sympathetic to the needs of all parents. The core message is that gDiapers are great for your baby (the value proposition) and great for the planet (notice that values are secondary in most of the messaging).

The Graham-Nyes believe that the primary question a parent will ask isn't, "What will this product do for the planet?" Instead it's, "Will this keep my baby dry and will this make my life easier?" At the base of the customer pyramid is comfort and functionality. As you move up the pyramid, gDiapers believes customers are secondarily interested in convenience, while the values message of eco-friendliness is at the top of the pyramid—the icing on the cake after the base needs have been met. Based upon this perception of its customer, it is essential that gDiapers speak to the fact that this product will make both the baby and the parent happy. A leaky diaper could make both very unhappy.

The folks at gDiapers could have chosen to lead with their environmental statement—both in terms of being good for the baby (lack of perfumes and polypropylene) and good for the planet. In some marketing channels, this may make sense, especially as they can advertise to the natural parenting market. But the reality is that almost all parents—whether they're eco-friendly or not—are extremely focused on their baby's well being as a foundational need.[10]

The real challenge for gDiapers will be to see how parents will balance the convenience benefits of disposables (since there's no need to occasionally clean out the "pants") with the eco-benefits of the gDiapers. If gDiapers can get parents to see diapers like they now see recycling (it's a little extra work to recycle but it provides tangible benefits to the planet and psychological benefits to the recycling customer), the product has a very bright future.

Reach Out to the Core Values of Your Bull's-Eye Customers

For a good example of reaching out, go to the Seventh Generation Web site. This producer of environmentally safe household products makes it very clear on its home page that it is speaking to the core values of its core customers, but it does so in an artful manner. There's a quote from the Great Law of the Iroquois Confederacy that helps explain the name of the company: "In our every deliberation we must consider the impact of our decisions on the next seven generations." There's stunning nature photography with people woven into the shots. There's a corporate responsibility report that outlines the company's economic, environmental, and social performance in terms of its impact on the community. And then there are different ways you can explore the site: "A Clean Home," "A Healthy Family," "A Safer World," "Making a Difference," "Our Products," and "About Us." You will find the site rich in information from nontoxic yard care to a discussion of global warming.[11]

Compare that with the giant household product company Procter & Gamble's home page. P&G's Web site has a more generic collection of categories that you can explore: "Products," "Company," "News," "Careers," "Investor," and "B2B Directory." While the company does offer on its home page two examples of socially responsible behavior (P&G's response to recent disasters and its "Live, Learn and Thrive" program focused on helping in the developing world),[12] the fact that "Products" shows up as its first category—whereas it shows up fifth for Seventh Generation—is subtle but telling. With the Seventh Generation site, if you share common core values with the company and you've reviewed all the sections of the site before coming to "Products," you don't need to be sold. You're already convinced that this is the right company for you.

Both of these companies compete in what is a relatively generic industry, yet Seventh Generation has chosen to distinguish itself by leading its marketing with a statement of its core values. In fact, Seventh Generation is clearly living its corporate mission by how it presents itself on its Web site: "We are committed to becoming the world's most trusted brand of authentic, safe, and environmentally responsible products for a healthy home. We are dedicated to setting the standard for superior service and to providing our customers with the resources and inspiration they need to make informed, responsible decisions."[13]

Ask yourself, "How generic is my product category?" It's a hard question to answer because most of us don't want to admit that our customers could see our product as interchangeable with our competitors'. The reality is if you are using coupons or other old-school methods of financial coercion as a significant means of trying to attract new customers, you might want to consider reaching out to the values of your customers instead.

Here's an example that illustrates how a big company can reach out to the core values of its customers. General Mills had historically used coupons as a means of marketing its cereals, but over time, it found that its customers no longer clipped coupons. General Mills came to realize that while its customers saw breakfast cereals as a relatively generic product category, its "bull's-eye" customers (mothers or, in some cases, fathers) were time starved (part of the reason they weren't clipping coupons). These parents felt guilty for not being able to contribute more to their children's schools in meaningful ways.

General Mills decided to create a Box Tops for Education program to address its core customers' core values. On the flaps of its cereal boxes, the company placed a logo that customers could clip and turn in to their schools. For each box top collected, General Mills makes a 10-cent donation to that school.

Billions of box tops have been collected over the years, representing millions of dollars donated to schools ($150 million since 1996—it is the company's largest strategic philanthropy effort).[14]

The average family might go through three boxes of cereal a week, which means (if they bought only General Mills cereals) they would earn thirty cents a week or fifteen dollars per year for their school. Logic would suggest that time-starved parents would rather write a small check annually to their school as opposed to collecting box tops and sending them in. But General Mills came to realize that this promotion gave parents a way to meaningfully (and rather easily) connect with their children and help out their community. It is truly a feel-good promotion because it makes customers feel like they're making a difference.[15]

What is meaningful to your bull's-eye customers? Seventh Generation's core customer is likely much more values driven than the typical General Mills customer, but both companies can score a marketing win by connecting with the core values of their customers.

As You Grow, Recognize That Your Message Needs to Resonate with a Wider Audience

What worked before may not work as your dartboard gets bigger and you have a larger audience. The *New York Times* featured a story about the values-driven Honest Tea company that made this point beautifully.[16]

Honest Tea is the nation's best-selling and fastest-growing organic bottled tea company. Seth Goldman started the company after working at the Calvert Group, a mutual fund firm that specializes in socially responsible investing. He created Honest Tea because he wanted to make a tea that wasn't so "cloyingly sweet." Initially, its core customers appreciated the value proposition of the unique taste but they also appreciated the organic values message behind the teas. As Honest Tea started getting wider distribution, it realized that some of its products were too esoteric for the more mainstream customer.

For example, in 2002, Honest Tea launched Haarlem Honeybush, a bottled, unsweetened, no-caffeine variety of tea made with ingredients from a South African farm that had backing from the U.S. Agency for International Development. This was a fairly ambitious agenda for a drink—and it didn't catch on. Most customers didn't know what honeybush was (an African shrub) and they weren't too sure where Haarlem was. Seth Goldman says this recognition that the broader market may not be as values-focused as thought has been an education for him. "That's something that the company and I have probably gone through an evolution on," he says, "We've probably had periods where we kind of overemphasized the mission."

In 2003, Honest Tea used this lesson to launch Peach-Oo-la-long, which was a sweeter tea (as compared to the unsweetened Haarlem Honeybush), contained a little caffeine, and featured not just a clear flavor promise (peach) but also Opus from the comic strip *Bloom County* on the label. Goldman sums it up this way, "We made it a much more accessible tea,"[17] which meant that it could cross over to the mainstream, which, in fact, it did.

The value proposition had to be more front and center for the more mainstream customer, but this product is still organic, has a caloric count far below soft drinks, and uses leaves from a Fair-Trade-Certified plantation in India. Honest Tea was able to find the perfect balance of communicating value and values.

If You're Purchased, Influence Your Parent

In the past few years, more and more multinational companies have gone shopping for socially responsible smaller companies to purchase. These huge companies realize that values are increasingly important in the decision-making process of customers. Furthermore, these companies acknowledge that rarely can they create an underdog brand in-house that will have the culture and values that many customers are looking for in the marketplace.

Hence, Coca-Cola purchases Odwalla and Unilever purchases Ben & Jerry's. Unfortunately, what often happens is the values proposition in the acquired underdog brand gets watered down after the acquisition occurs, which is bad news for the acquired company, the acquiring company, and the customer.

The Culting of Brands author Douglas Atkin says, "What ideologically based companies do is make a contract with their customer. If they break that contract, customers will reject them as fervently as they [supported them]."[18] The net result can be poisonous to the brand. But this doesn't have to happen. In fact, a socially responsible company can influence its parent.

Aveda was created in 1978 as a high-end organic cosmetics brand. When Estée Lauder purchased the company in 1997, many feared that Aveda would have to alter its more expensive, plant-based manufacturing process. On the contrary, Aveda has continued to push the envelope in terms of improving its product by sustainably sourcing organic products globally and dramatically increasing its use of postconsumer recycled content in its product containers. Furthermore, Aveda is influencing its parent by means of lab research, such as the study suggesting that hair is not a dead material, which is a long-held belief in the traditional cosmetics world, dictating the accepted formulation of chemicals as safe for use in hair products. Estée Lauder is now looking at some of its environmental practices to bring it in line with Aveda. Between 2002 and 2005, Aveda doubled its revenues by appealing to both the fashionable and the eco-sensitive customer.[19]

Similarly, Fetzer Vineyards is the sixth largest premium winery in the United States, selling 3.5 million cases of wine a year. Every single acre owned by Fetzer is certified organic, and the winery is considered a "zero waste" business by the state of California. It was purchased in the early 1990s by alcohol giant Brown-Forman (Jack Daniels, Southern Comfort).

At first, there was some concern that the parent company might not appreciate Fetzer's unique values-driven approach to product development and marketing, but recently Brown-Forman launched its first chairman's conference on sustainability. The parent company has publicly said that it sees Fetzer as a laboratory of what's new and how its brands can use eco-values as a means of attracting a loyal customer base.[20]

Many socially responsible entrepreneurs raise money from investors with the perspective that some day there will be a liquidity event (an initial public offering in the stock market, a sale to another company) that will provide their investors the primary return on their investment. It is easy to understand why these entrepreneurs may have mixed emotions when they know their values-driven "baby" may ultimately have a parent that has different values with respect to how to bring up baby. Aveda and Fetzer prove that a smaller values-driven company can have an even bigger positive impact on the world when it influences its corporate parent to operate and market itself in a more socially responsible manner.

NEW SEASONS MARKET

COMMUNICATING VALUE AND VALUES

At New Seasons Market, value and values reinforce one another. By looking at what drives customers' choices about where they do their weekly grocery shopping, New Seasons designed a value and values proposition to deeply resonate with the customers' primary decision drivers. These drivers include availability of the items that customers want, the ease of being able to get all of their grocery needs in one place, competitive pricing that provides great value for the grocery dollar, and healthy food and friendly customer service. New Seasons also connects with customers' values drivers. The values drivers answer a primary need for the core customer group and are important secondary drivers for a much larger mainstream customer group. New Seasons' values proposition invites customers to support the local economy, demonstrate environmental responsibility with their grocery dollars, support important community and social priorities, and experience a strong sense of connection and community.

We have already talked a great deal about New Seasons' values proposition. So here we'd like to expand a bit on the value proposition that connects with a primary driver for both the traditional core organic and environmentally oriented customer and the much larger base of customers who live within the trade area of each New Seasons store. The availability of delicious, nutritious, and high quality food at competitive prices is a core and primary customer driver. New Seasons puts significant effort into sourcing a wide variety of produce, meats, dairy, and other fresh grocery products, as well as a huge assortment of wines, prepared foods, and other specialty grocery items, many of which are organic and natural. At the same time, New Seasons stocks thousands of the most popular basic grocery products that the average household purchases. From soda pop and cereals to instant and frozen foods, it provides a mainstream–organic and natural product mix to meet the full grocery needs of its customers.

An equally important driver is a pricing strategy that establishes New Seasons as a primary weekly grocery store rather than a specialty stop. New Seasons makes sure that its prices on an item-by-item basis are competitive with conventional supermarkets. Select a whole organic chicken or a quart of local organic strawberries—the New Seasons prices are generally the same as at a conventional supermarket. Select a gallon of 2 percent milk and a loaf of sliced sourdough sandwich bread—the prices are generally the same as at a conventional store. Select a box of frosted flakes and a six-pack of Diet Coke—again, the prices are comparable. "We are not a fancy pants place," says New Seasons Market's Brian Rohter. "We want all our neighbors to be able to shop here and we price our items accordingly. You can shop here on a budget as well as you can at our national chain competitors."[21] Rather than stocking a small selection, charging a premium for conventional grocery items, and being thought of by customers as a specialty store, New Seasons has made its prices competitive and comparable to a regular supermarket.

Another primary driver for food shoppers is good food—delicious food of high quality. New Seasons knows that many customers have an increasing desire for healthy and organic foods, so it seeks out the largest variety of organic and natural products and provides customers with lots of information so they can make informed purchasing choices. It also recognizes the value of conveying that its food is delicious, beautiful, and abundant. Wander the aisles of a New Seasons store and you will be impressed not only by the abundance and beauty of the displays but also by the opportunity to taste, sample, and experience the food. Shopping at New Seasons is really like attending a delicious weekly food festival.

Ultimately, customers choose to do their weekly grocery shopping at a place where they know they can find what they need, that is convenient and fun, that provides a wide selection of food they know is good for them, and where their

weekly grocery bill is comparable to any mainline supermarket. They love to do their weekly shopping where they can
connect to their neighborhoods, help the environment, and
support the local economy. Combined, New Seasons Market's
■ value and values propositions resonate with customers.[22]

Communicate Value and Values

As the saying goes, communication is everything. All companies
should ensure that the value of their product is conveyed as simply and clearly as possible. But socially responsible business
leaders need to take this one step further—and for some it's a big
step. Sharing your values is a smart business decision but one
that must be approached with real commitment and clarity of
purpose.

Now let's take an even deeper look into the heart of your
customer and explore how emotions take center stage in building your relationship.

Emotion trumps data

PRACTICE 7: CONNECT WITH THE HEART FIRST, MIND SECOND

Chip remembers the first time he saw the Clif Bar ad that depicts a poignant photo of founder Gary Erickson leaning against his father, Clif, as they walk through a forest (with Gary on his bike). The ad copy headline read: "IN 1990, MY SON TURNED 33 AND MOVED INTO A GARAGE." It went on to tell the story from Clif's perspective of what it's been like seeing his son, the adventurer, grow up and start Clif Bar, naming the company after his dad. In tiny italics down in the lower corner, the ad showed three Clif Bars and the note "every flavor made with certified organic ingredients," along with the Web site address where the reader could learn more about the product.[1]

That ad stuck with Chip and is a great example of how the majority of customers tend to favor heart over mind when they think of companies and products. Many studies hypothesize how successful brands connect first instinctually with their customers and then intellectually. In 2002, researchers at the University of Florida analyzed data from 23,168 people in thirteen different product categories and found that emotions are nearly twice as important as knowledge in buying decisions across all kinds of industries.[2]

Saatchi & Saatchi Advertising CEO Kevin Roberts writes in his book *Lovemarks,* "If the emotion centers of our brain are damaged in some way, we don't just lose the ability to laugh or cry, we lose the ability to make decisions. And neurologist Donald Calne puts it brilliantly: 'The essential difference between emotion and reason is that emotion leads to action while reason leads to conclusion.'"[3] Of course, it takes action—not conclusion—for your customer to buy your product.

This makes common sense. Building a relationship with a customer isn't all that different from dating. When we meet someone we find highly attractive, most of us don't begin by analyzing physical and emotional attributes to determine why we have a magnetic pull in his or her direction. If we do, it usually means we're sitting on our hands and not taking action. Ironically, the analysis itself may even reduce the intensity of our feelings toward him or her. In our personal lives, our emotions influence our actions.

Marketing researchers have come to realize that what people think is less predictable than what they feel when it comes to what products they'll buy. Ed Keller, president of Roper ASW, says demographic data or traditional customer surveys can correctly guess what kind of car an individual will buy only 18 percent of the time. But "when you combine people's attitudes, behaviors, life stages and values" (psychographics), Keller suggests, "you can predict 82 percent of the time what car a person will buy next."[4] Once again, people's approaches to making personal decisions and their approaches to making customer decisions are more similar than marketing professionals have historically thought.

When it comes to the more conscious customer, Marc Gobe, author of *Emotional Branding,* says, "Based on the products they are using, customers get permission to express themselves and be socially responsible. Emotional branding provides the means and methodology for connecting products to the customer in an emotionally profound way. It focuses on the most compelling aspect of the human character: the desire to transcend material satisfaction and experience emotional fulfillment. A brand is uniquely situated to achieve this, because it can tap into the aspirational drives which underlie human motivation."[5] It sounds like Mr. Gobe has been reading some Maslow!

Quite often, socially responsible companies use values-driven messages to connect with the hearts of their customers—and some really push the envelope. Think of fashion icon Kenneth Cole, known best for his ads that question everything from our government's choices to our own. Or the house of Benetton, the clothier that changed the face of advertising by first featuring multicultural models in its Colors campaign and later addressing a litany of social ills, paving the way for Cole and others. Benetton and Cole are renowned for producing provocative political and social justice ads—conceived to bathe their brands in a positive emotional light—with the explicit intention of manifesting change through commerce.

As we suggested in the last chapter, there can be a risk when a company invests too much in the values brand image and not enough in the value of the product. Furthermore, emotionally driven marketing has the risk of looking manipulative. Many customers have tired of having their heart tugged at by some company trying to sell them something. Balance is a good thing, not just with value and values, but also in terms of how you market to both the left and the right brain. We'll discuss some of the questions you can ask yourself and approaches to achieving this balance in chapter 9.

Naomi Klein, author of *No Logo,* sums up one of the risks of developing a branding campaign that doesn't have strong underpinnings: "In many ways, branding is the Achilles' heel of the corporate world. The more these companies shift to being all about brand meaning and brand image, the more vulnerable they are to attacks on image."[6] She's got a good point.

Compare athletic gear giant Nike and home design leader Ikea. Neither are strangers to controversy, yet the mud stuck to Nike, not Ikea. Look at the brand values to find out why. The Ikea brand is about the value of equality—democratizing good furniture for better living. That was the emotional "brand truth" it was communicating to customers. On the contrary, Nike's values center on the individual thrill of crushing the competition while living up to your potential.

When Ikea was accused of supporting child labor through its overseas sourcing of rugs, it apologized and worked with UNICEF to develop a standards commission dedicated to eradicating child labor in the manufacture of household goods. When Nike faced a similar situation, it got covered in mud partly because its brand image felt less warm and fuzzy. "Just Do It" went from being an asset about the power of the individual to being a perceived liability about the power of multinationals. To Nike's credit, it made a commitment to expand its corporate responsibility division to seventy people, which ultimately helped it to switch its labor practices and improve its brand image.[7]

But Naomi Klein's point is well taken. Emotionally driven marketing is powerful—and dangerous. Here are a few tips that will help assure that your first date with your customer becomes a long-term relationship:

- Be real—Authenticity that's grounded in reality works, but false sentiment doesn't. Don't try to pull at the heartstrings just because it feels like it will win you more customers. No one likes dating a sweet talker for long.

- Manage expectations—Don't promise the world. Is your product good enough to back up the emotional buildup you've created? Remember, both in dating and in marketing, disappointment is the natural result of badly managed expectations.

- Follow feelings with facts—In the Clif Bar ad, Chip was initially won over by the emotion, but he was also given the option of going to the Web site to learn more about the product. Poetry can carry a date for only so long—at some point, I want to learn a little more about you.

How do you go about connecting with the heart first? Start by asking yourself how your customer perceives your brand. You may think you don't have a brand because your company has just four customers and annual sales of $50,000. But every company has a brand just like every individual has a personality. And the way your customers perceive your brand will go a long way to determining how emotionally connected they are to you.

Core Applications

We recommend four steps that will help your brand make a deeper emotional connection with your customers:

1. Develop your brand story.
2. Develop avenues to connect with your customer in emotionally authentic ways.
3. Package the product in a way that creates an emotional response.
4. Use your historical roots to create an emotional connection.

Develop Your Brand Story

Stories are sticky. As humans, we're wired to remember narratives, whereas we'll forget the details of a PowerPoint presentation by tomorrow. Stories translate information into emotion, and the best stories stick to your brain and your heart.

In a *Fast Company* magazine article titled "The Top 10 Brand Storytellers," Karen Post surmised, "The goal of a brand is to connect to the market with emotion and relevance. Make it an engaging, enjoyable experience; have a premise and a point; and be memorable. Applying storytelling principles to a brand development strategy simply makes the journey more efficient and effective."[8] (In the article, two of the companies highlighted are SRBs we have featured, ShoreBank and Kimpton.) The brands with the strongest emotional connection with their customers—like Apple, Jet Blue, and Harley-Davidson—are masters at storytelling. They're so good at creating a story that the bulk of the storytelling responsibility is left to their cheerleading customers.

What are the elements of a good story? It should be short and simple. It should be interesting and worth talking about. It should reinforce a key pillar of the product. It should be able to be told in story form. For example, most of us have heard the story about the woman who returned a tire to Nordstrom and received a refund even though the department store doesn't sell tires.[9] This story fits all four elements, with the key pillar being Nordstrom's strong reputation for service and liberal return/refund policy. A good story had also better be true. To date, no one has refuted the Nordstrom myth, even though when we first heard the story, it did have a bit of a big fish tale ring to it.

Another way to tell your story is to look at your origins. Dan Storper of Putumayo World Music tells the story of how he came about the company name. Putumayo is an area in southern Columbia that he loved to visit (and, in fact, this story has appeared in many articles that have been written about Putumayo). The first time he arrived there was during one of its carnival celebrations, and he marveled at the homegrown music found in such a naturally beautiful setting.

He says, "What we've done with Putumayo World Music is an attempt to try and help people travel the world. To let them explore other cultures and have a taste of the mystery and appeal of World Music. To let them discover how by being melodic and upbeat it helps people rise above their daily problems. It makes you feel good and becomes a positive element that has been created in another culture. I believe it is the positive side of the human spirit, and that music is one of the positive elements that human beings create. I also believe that, ultimately, the same thing drives people everywhere. That is, to try and find ways to make their lives happier and more meaningful. Unfortunately, there aren't that many things that do it. But music is one of those things."[10]

The story of how Dan came up with the name of his business and the soul that is behind the business (which is obvious when you see the artful compact disc covers and packaging—also representative of our third application in this chapter) creates an emotional connection with customers. In fact, that brings up one last element of socially responsible storytelling: it should suggest a greater good.

Ethos Water is based on a powerfully simple concept: water for water. Ethos is a for-profit company that has linked its product, bottled water, to the cause of providing safe water to those in need. It is another good example—as we showed in the last chapter—that a generic product has an even better chance of creating a values-driven message. While the Ethos story is simple, the origins of the company help make the emotional connection—and, like Clif Bar, the story is available to customers when they visit the Ethos Web site.

The idea behind Ethos was born out of the direct personal experience of founder Peter Thum. In 2001, Peter worked on a consulting project in South Africa. During this time, he witnessed the extraordinary suffering of impoverished children, whose life prospects were diminished due to the lack of safe drinking water. Peter and his friend Jonathan Greenblatt launched the company in 2002 with the intent of helping fund water projects (with the organization WaterPartners) in the developing world. In fact, Ethos is currently supporting water projects in Bangladesh, the Democratic Republic of Congo, Ethiopia, Honduras, India, and Kenya.[11]

But the storytelling goes back to the roots of the company. Jonathan Greenblatt explains, "We were running the company from my son's bedroom. We were building one store at a time, delivering water out of the back of a beat-up borrowed Volvo station wagon and created our little company, which was mainly bankrolled by the two of us for a long time. We funded it with our credit cards and savings accounts."[12]

Not only was the Ethos story interesting to its growing collection of customers—Starbucks took notice and bought the company in 2005. Starbucks joined in Ethos's goal of supporting water projects to the tune of donating a minimum of $250,000 in 2005 and an additional $1 million by the end of fiscal year 2006.[13]

Telling a good story can build an emotional connection with your customers, and it can also make you an attractive acquisition target (if that's what you're looking for) since larger companies are desperately in need of connecting to authentic feel-good stories that make a difference in the world.

How do you get started with your storytelling? Consider gathering your leadership team in a room and looking at your company's roots, its aspirations, or a particularly compelling customer experience that can be articulated to the world. Ask each person to talk to two loyal customers about how they describe the company, brand, product, or service to their friends. See what's consistent in their messaging and start to build a story that you can use in all of your communications with the world: on your Web site, in your brochures, in your press releases, in your company orientation with new employees. Your brand story is how you see yourself and how you want the world to see you.

Develop Avenues to Connect with Your Customer in Emotionally Authentic Ways

In *Lovemarks*, Kevin Roberts asks a provocative question: "How do you get intimate with customers without being invasive or insincere?"[14] This is such a refreshing question in today's world of commoditized brands, where everything feels standardized, distant, and lacking in personal touch. Get this question right and you'll build a fiercely loyal customer base.

Roberts continues, "Intimacy requires an understanding of what matters to people at a very deep level. And that understanding means that you have to be prepared to reveal yourself as well. Reveal your true feelings. Not standard behavior for most corporations!"[15]

Chip had a sense of this when he launched Joie de Vivre's new Hotel Vitale on San Francisco Bay in 2005. He felt that there was a niche in the marketplace—what he called the "post-W, pre–Four Seasons customer"—that was underserved by the current product offerings. This hotel guest had outgrown the hip and trendily exclusive W Hotel experience but wasn't yet ready for the formality and old-school luxury of the Four Seasons. He felt this customer was looking for a hotel that was a unique juxtaposition of stylish yet humble, professionally minded yet progressive. In a world full of multinational chain hotels with no authentic voice, Chip wanted to connect emotionally with his customers. How do you do that when, as the owner, you can't be at the front desk twenty-four hours a day?

Chip's launch team created a thirty-two page *Vitale* magazine that colorfully articulates the best hidden treasures Vitale guests should seek out in San Francisco's Embarcadero waterfront neighborhood. And at the front of this attractive, magazine-like publication is a photo of Chip with his personal note that says: "What's truly important in life? Is it the fact that you've traded-up to the BMW 7-series from the 3-series or is it the collection of memories and experiences that you've treated yourself to over the course of your lifetime? Many of us have come to recognize that our material possessions aren't what sustain us. Instead, what's significant are the daily little vignettes we create in our lives."

The letter goes on to say that this magazine is a "customized instruction manual for creating memories," and it articulates, in a from-the-heart manner, just how important this hotel is to Chip and to his company. He even goes on to include his e-mail address in the letter and encourages guests to "track [him] down." What's the result of trying to make this emotional connection? Each month, Chip gets dozens of e-mails from primarily ecstatic guests and strikes up an e-mail relationship with each of them. When he gets the occasional dissatisfied guest who wants to express his or her disappointment, Chip is able to make that emotional connection, too—as well as engage his hotel staff in creating solutions for that guest. In sum, in an anonymous world of hotels that want you to think of them as your "home away from home," isn't it nice to know whose home you're staying in and what kind of values it has?

Big companies can also engage in this kind of customer intimacy. Hasbro was a big toy company with a bit of a tired image. It realized that children were playing video games at earlier ages. This meant they were no longer playing Hasbro board games and that they were losing some connection with their parents since few parents play video games. Research showed that the sooner parents started playing board games with their children, the more likely the children would continue to play board games. And, of course, the net result of this might be a more communicative and closer family.

In order to market this idea, Hasbro designed an ad campaign that spoke directly to parents. The goal was to influence parents to begin playing board games with their children at three years old and make it easier for the parents to choose an appropriate game to play. This was done by branding all of the Hasbro preschool games that met the criteria of being educational under the umbrella of My First Games. To reinforce the educational elements, such as counting, color recognition, and taking turns, Dr. Sylvia Rimm, a leading child psychologist, was enlisted as a spokesperson and advocate for the brand. She appeared on every game package to help parents recognize the benefits of the game.

With the campaign slogan "The best part of playing is playing together," the ads depicted a parent and a child giggling and hugging while playing a board game. The words that inspired the ad campaign were "Daddy, come and play a game with me." This ad campaign had the highest positive customer ratings in Hasbro's history and proved equally successful in the market.[16]

Creating an emotional connection with your customers has a lot to do with getting inside their hearts and speaking to their values. The more you behave like a friend or facilitator, the more likely your customer will keep coming back for more.

Package the Product in a Way That Creates an Emotional Response

Some product categories have the potential to evoke emotional responses more than others. What emotions come up for you when you think of tea? Mystery and exoticism? Relaxation? Doilies and crumpets? Historically in America, tea was defined by Lipton and Bigelow and was a rather boring product category.

But then along came new brands like the Republic of Tea, Numi Tea, and Tazo that helped shift the whole idea of tea in Americans' minds to being something almost spiritual.

Each of these new brands has tried to tell a rather mystical story about tea. Back in chapter 2, we talked about Tazo, a company that took its name from ancient times. The name means "river of life" in the Romany Gypsy language and was used as a toast to life by ancient Greeks. The tea company was founded in 1994 with the idea that it was going to "reincarnate" tea.[17]

Steve Seto, the vice president of branding for Tazo, says, "It's a very modern notion of spirituality that, like the product itself, borrows from multiple spiritual and cultural influences— a simple, yet textured idea that customers respond to emotionally. It invites them in and allows them to interpret the brand on their own terms. It's sort of like yoga: some do yoga just for the physical benefits while others take it to a deeper level and are rewarded with personal, spiritual benefits that the practice offers. Our positioning works to take people to this deeper place, to convey that Tazo does have the ability to make you feel a certain way (soothed, refreshed, revitalized, or restored)."[18]

We think Tazo's packaging is the icing on the cake for this emotional connection. The Tazo brand is built around spiritual images, using icons that resemble language from long ago and far away—a combination of elements that seem to draw equally from *The Lord of the Rings* and Hinduism. Featuring unique tea blends with names like Zen, Tazo creates a holistic impression that says "slow down, experience this, you will be enriched." In essence, the emotional message is this "inexpensive, little product will provide you a quick escape from your crazy life." And the result is that Tazo has continued growing market share to the point that Starbucks (yes, again) acquired the company in 1999.[19]

How are you packaging your product or service? Ask what your customers are really looking for. It may not be immediately obvious. The obvious answer for tea drinkers is that they're looking for a warm beverage. But in reality, traditional tea drinkers may be seeking civility while postmodern tea drinkers may be looking for an escape. Once you've discovered this underlying customer emotional motivation, you can package your product or service to address this message.

Use Your Historical Roots to Create an Emotional Connection

The use of nostalgia can be anything but socially responsible. Most American companies that use nostalgia often do so in a fashion that can feel regressive, not progressive. That's why when it's done by a socially responsible company, it can make an even more profound emotional impact on the conscious customer.

Birkenstock has a venerable history dating back more than 225 years to Germany. Margot Fraser introduced the shoe brand in America (becoming its exclusive distributor here) in 1966, and it quickly became associated with the new youth movement. The Northern California headquarters, the funky and casual look, and the adherence to green principles all created a branding that could be called crunchy or granola-y. Those customers who looked beyond that veneer found that Birkenstock always adhered to a recyclable tradition. The shoe design considers the entire life cycle of the shoe from the source of materials and the reduction of waste to energy-efficient manufacturing and the repair, reuse, and recyclability of the finished product.

Yet this mellow counterculture image was starting to weigh on the company, as the average age of its customers was far higher than for its competitors. Like many brands that are forty years old (in terms of the launch in the United States), Birkenstock's customers were starting to die off. In order for the company to reach out to a younger audience with its marketing, it had to move from hippie to hip without being inconsistent with its heritage of turning out comfortable, environmentally sound footwear.

Birkenstock hired Yves Behar and his company, fuseproject, a cutting-edge industrial design and branding firm, to create a new brand tailored for younger urban creatives. This new brand (launched as the Architect Collection and now part of the Footprints line) stayed true to some of the roots of Birkenstock: more width in the shoe and more space for the toes than is typical, as well as using biodegradable or recycled materials. At the same time, this new shoe line was meant to be much more elegant, modern, and, dare we say, fashionable than anything Birkenstock had ever delivered to the market before.

The net result is a shoe that speaks to young people whose parents, or maybe even grandparents, are Birkenstock enthusiasts. The new shoe line was launched at the Museum of Modern Art in San Francisco and the Kartell Museo in New York's Soho district. For the launch events, a large architectural piece—a gigantic chandelier made of some eighty dangling Birkenstock shoes—floated above those coming to the parties. The Footprints design has won fuseproject numerous design awards.

This example proves that a company can be true to its ergonomic and ecological roots while still innovating to meet the customer's changing tastes and needs. In story terms, Yves Behar and fuseproject reinterpreted Birkenstock's original message of reliability and "greenness" for a new generation of stylish, ecology-minded people. Just like Hush Puppies became cool again in the last few years, so did Birkenstocks.[20]

If purchasing is a convenient form of activism, consider your company's socially responsible roots and use that connection to the past to inspire your current customers to continue to stay loyal to your brand.

CONNECT WITH THE HEART FIRST, MIND SECOND

New Seasons Market clearly recognizes that the emotion and experience of delicious food and great, personalized customer service are more memorable to customers than lists of information. At the same time, New Seasons has also made a distinct value proposition that supports customers' desire to get information about where their food comes from, how it is grown, how it is produced, and its impact on the environment. New Seasons strives to blend these complementary emotional and data needs. It connects customers to the emotion that comes from the taste and beauty of food and that is conveyed by the real stories and real opportunities to meet and engage with farmers, ranchers, fishers, cheese makers, and winemakers. It connects customers to immediate availability of detailed information to answer questions and to back up claims. But it is the emotion of storytelling that is memorable and that serves as a gateway for many customers to the more detailed information.

New Seasons serves as a platform for vendors—the growers and producers of food—to connect with their ultimate customers. In the process of connecting producers and customers, New Seasons helps decommodify food and tells a powerful story. Visit New Seasons prior to Easter and meet the young man offering samples of incredible lamb kabobs and marinated barbequed lamb. He invites a conversation, and you learn how he plans to take over his family farm, how he and his family manage their land, and about his father's marinade recipe that he is happy to share with you. Go to New Seasons and meet ranchers who are members of the Oregon Country Beef cooperative and hear the stories of their family farms while you taste some of the best beef in the world. Go to New Seasons when the chinook salmon are in season and meet the fisherman whose line catches salmon off the Oregon coast. From CEO Brian Rohter's perspective, "The weekend events where our customers meet the cheese makers, fishers, or farmers are unforgettable, have a lasting impact on the way city people view their rural neighbors, and create brand loyalty in a way that Procter & Gamble can only dream about."[21] Each story gives New Seasons' customers a deeper connection to the food they eat and to the place in which they live. Each story helps create a relationship with a bit of romance and a lot of respect for the food that we are eating. Each story gives customers something that they are excited to talk about and share at the home dinner table or at the party where they bring a dish to share.

By contrast, has anyone ever shared a story with you about how exciting it was to pick out a piece of meat from the freezer that was clad in Styrofoam and plastic wrap? This inspires no story. Whereas New Seasons Market, by highlighting its vendors and the story behind the food, has created a legitimate emotional connection that opens the doorway for customers to seek additional knowledge and information.[22]

■ Emotion trumps data.

Connect with the Heart

Customers prefer to buy from someone they like and admire. They want to build a relationship with you; therefore it makes sense for you to create an emotional connection with them through both your marketing strategy and your tactics. If you develop a compelling brand story and a great product or service, there's no doubt that you'll create big word of mouth.

Now we're going to show you how to empower people to be messengers for your brand and how to build a community around your business.

Build a community

PRACTICE 8: EMPOWER PEOPLE
AS MESSENGERS

Imagine an experiment with a pair of twins walking down the street in the same direction—one of the twins on one side of the street and the other on the opposite side. One wears a T-shirt with the Dell logo emblazoned on it, while the other wears a shirt with an Apple logo. Over the course of walking a few blocks on a crowded city street, how many familiar reactions (a wink, a nod, a smile) will the Apple twin get as compared to the Dell twin? While both are well-respected technology companies, Apple has a cultlike following and has created a community of cheerleaders who live and breathe the brand. And, no doubt, this community is more likely to nod or smile to one of its brethren.

Building a community of believers is one of the best pieces of marketing advice we can give to any businessperson. Keeping this advice in mind will undoubtedly serve both your financial and your values aspirations. According to consulting giant McKinsey & Company, about two-thirds of all economic activity in the United States is influenced by peoples' shared opinions about a product, brand, or service.[1] It's logical that the people who are most likely to share an opinion are the true believers who feel part of a brand's community. And, of course, word-of-mouth recommendations are not just more influential—and considered to be more trustworthy—but they're dramatically less expensive than any other form of marketing. More and more, "source credibility" defines whether your potential customers believe what they hear about your product or whether they take it with a grain of salt.

What if you had to tell your story nine times before your best friend acknowledged what you were saying? For one, you'd probably pick a new best friend. But that's a good way of looking at the inherent flaws in traditional advertising. Conventional wisdom suggests that it takes nine impressions for a potential customer to retain the information in an ad. One good story from a friend far outweighs the potential of nine expensive ads.

This chapter focuses on how you build a community—a credible source—that's committed to your business. That community is larger than just your most loyal customers. Good word of mouth also comes from employees, strategic partners, industry observers, and the media. Engage all of these constituencies and you have the makings of what author Douglas Atkin and others now refer to as a cult brand.[2]

Cult brands are not the only brands that receive positive word of mouth, but they are the ones that create the greatest bang for the buck. So let's study what makes a cult brand and how it engages its followers by creating a sense of community.

What makes a cult brand? There are four common characteristics that you'll find in any cult brand: (1) a differentiated product, (2) an empowered employee and customer base that appreciates being part of something outside the mainstream, (3) a renegade or underdog message, and (4) an easy ability to join the community.

Dell is a commodity while Apple is differentiated. Commodities speak to the mainstream and don't create cult brands.

Cult brands emerge when a company launches an unusual product or service that captures the fascination of a certain niche of customers in the marketplace. For example, the reintroduced Volkswagen Beetle and Mini Cooper created huge fervor from a segment of car buyers. How many people marry their car? Mazda Miata is a bit of a cult brand that led 250 Miata owners to a mass ceremony and party in which an Episcopal priest spoke the following words in the Pocono Mountains, "By the power vested in me, I pronounce you are . . . car and driver."[3]

Enthusiastic employees and customers who feel emotionally associated with this kind of differentiated brand are a powerful cornerstone of a cult brand. Cult branders know that they're not just selling a product or service but they're connecting with the dreams, passions, and aspirations of their employees and customers. The power of association or the sense of belonging is a deep need in all humans and one that cult brands do a wonderful job of satisfying.

Most cult brands start with a shoestring budget and a David versus Goliath worldview. The combination of that underdog philosophy with a renegade message or product means that these in-the-know customers recognize how important they are to the company's future success. The fastest way to create evangelical customers is to make them feel that their voice is heard—and essential.

A simple example of this comes from the origins of the popular British company Innocent Drinks. Three young blokes decided they wanted to quit their boring jobs in advertising and management consulting and start a smoothie business. They set up a stand at a small music festival in London and put up a big sign that read: "Do you think we should give up our jobs to make these smoothies?" They put out one trash bin that said Yes and one that said No and asked people to discard their empty bottles into the right bin. They got very quick and detailed customer feedback, and now, just a few years later, they've built their company into one of the UK's best-known socially responsible cult brands.[4]

Finally, the last common characteristic of cult brands is that each brand welcomes everyone who's interested into its community. Harley-Davidson appeals to all types and has created their well-known Harley Owners Group (H.O.G.) as a means for Harley owners to connect with each other and share their love of the product. This is easier to do when you have a lifestyle-driven product that naturally encourages a gathering of community.

The Internet is the perfect medium for furthering the conversation between companies and their most enthusiastic customers. Check out any marketing-savvy, socially responsible company's Web site and we bet you'll find many ways to engage with the community that orbits around that company or brand. One of our favorites is Clif Bar's Web site, where you can click on "Live" and read adventure stories from Clif Bar employees around the world as well as experiences from Clif Bar customers. For those Clif Bar cheerleaders who want to participate, there's a list under "Play" of events, Team Clif sports activities, and information on the Marathon Pace Team. It also has a blog that's populated with the Clif Bar community talking about everything from the state of the world to the state of Clif's newest product launch.

Let's take a closer look at one company that is a role model for creating community. More than forty years ago, Patagonia founder Yvon Chouinard produced his first mail-order catalog, a one-page mimeographed sheet of adventure gear advising potential customers not to expect fast delivery during climbing season. Patagonia is now an international organization with annual sales that exceed a quarter-billion dollars, but it still feels like a funky, homegrown little company.[5]

Does Patagonia have a differentiated product? In Yvon Chouinard's manifesto, *Let My People Go Surfing: The Education of a Reluctant Businessman,* he writes, "Striving to make the best quality product is the reason we got into business in the first place. We are a product-driven company, and without a tangible product there would obviously be no business . . . because we had a history of making the best climbing tools in the world, tools that your life is dependent on, we couldn't be satisfied making second-best clothing."[6] Chip can vouch for that as he still has a Patagonia pullover jacket that he bought nearly twenty years ago, and it's actually become more and more comfortable with each passing year.

It's not just a matter of Patagonia creating the best product, but it also has a stated goal of causing "no unnecessary harm." In the 1990s, Patagonia's managers embarked on an effort to understand the life cycle impacts of the four major fibers used in its products: polyester, nylon, cotton, and wool. What they found surprised them as they learned that conventionally grown cotton had as much of a negative impact as synthetic fibers and wool. The company took more than one-third of its employees, as well as many of its suppliers, on a tour of cotton fields to make it clear why Patagonia had to make the expensive switch to using only organic cotton in the production of its clothing.

Once this decision was made—years before other, much larger companies disclosed their "dirty laundry"—Patagonia wrote in its next catalog, "everything we do pollutes." It unveiled its plan to change production methods and hinted of a cost implication for taking this environmentally responsible step. Patagonia's openness about the negative impact of its production created a high level of trust among its employees and managers. It definitely further engaged the 20 percent of its customers (based upon Patagonia's market research) whose buying patterns are heavily influenced by the values of the company from whom they purchase.[7] In chapter 9, we will further explore the power of authenticity and why socially responsible businesses choose to expose themselves.

Does Patagonia have an empowered employee and customer base that feels different? Patagonia's employee retention is four times better than the industry averages for retail companies, so clearly it has happy employees. To get a flavor of the way Patagonia uses its Web site to connect with its customers, visit the company's site. Click on "Our Culture" and you'll get a taste of the unique and quirky culture that defines the company. You can meet "Patagoniacs" who are product testers. Click on one of the ten people featured and find out about the adventure passions of these folks and how Patagonia's products help them experience a more full-bodied life.

Or click on "Sports We Do" and you'll find reflections on nine different sports (from alpine climbing to fly fishing) from some of Patagonia's employees as well as recommended clothing systems. The Patagonia community is deeply woven into the fabric of the company and has an enormous influence on the products that Patagonia creates.

Does Patagonia have a renegade message? Yvon Chouinard's book title certainly has a renegade spirit to it. On Patagonia's Web site under "Enviro Action," you can read about how you can make a difference regarding global warming or the Arctic National Wildlife Refuge. In 2004, Patagonia's customers sent fifteen thousand letters to President George Bush asking him to take out the four dams on the Snake River that were key to restoring salmon to that river system.

Patagonia's message has infused how it uses its catalog and Web site in its marketing. Over the years, Yvon writes, "We have come upon a balance we find just about ideal: 55 percent product content and 45 percent devoted to message—essays, stories, and image photos. Whenever we have edged that content toward increased product presentation, we have actually experienced a decrease in sales."[8]

Does Patagonia make it easy to join its community? In so many ways. For example, it puts a notice in its catalog asking customers and photographers to "capture a Patagoniac" in the midst of adventure using the company's products. The company was inundated with photos that became catalog content and helped customers feel like they were a part of the Patagonia culture (certainly more authentic than merely hiring an expensive model). Customers are also encouraged to participate in adventure events in far-flung places.

Since 1985, Patagonia has pledged 1 percent of its annual sales to organizations that are helping to preserve and restore the natural environment. The company has awarded nearly $20 million in grants to domestic and international grassroots groups that are making a difference in their local communities. More recently, Patagonia helped create "1% For The Planet," an alliance of two hundred businesses that have committed to donating 1 percent of their annual revenues to environmental causes. This is just one more way for Patagonia customers to feel like they are part of the unique community that orbits around this company.

As a cult brand, how does Patagonia approach the subject of marketing? The company has three general guidelines that define its promotional efforts:

1. "Our charter is to inspire and educate rather than promote."
2. "We would rather earn credibility than buy it. The best resources for us are the word-of-mouth recommendations from a friend or favorable comments in the press."
3. "We advertise only as a last resort."

Based upon this promotional strategy, Patagonia estimates it receives press coverage that would be comparable to about $7 million in annual advertising costs.[9]

The company has learned through trial and error how to develop successful promotional campaigns. From Patagonia's learning, we've been able to identify three steps the company takes to support its community's ability to spread word of mouth and connect with the company:

Step 1: Learn where your word of mouth comes from. The company's marketing team uses online and e-mail surveys to understand more about their customers' behavior and opinions. What it initially found was that about half of Patagonia customers eventually recommend the brand to others but that it takes some time before this word of mouth kicks in. It takes a while for customers to realize how durable the products are, and customers don't have enough opportunities to engage with the brand (given the low-key advertising and the fact that fewer than twenty retail stores are in the United States). This research also uncovered that the most evangelical customers were those who knew the most about the company's core values. The result of this research was for Patagonia to step up its messaging on its Web site and in its catalog and to provide as many means as possible for customers to interact with the brand.

Step 2: Develop cross-channel customer visibility and interaction. Patagonia has various distribution channels: its own stores, its Web site, its catalog, and its wholesale business in other stores. Prior to doing the research in Step 1, these four distribution channels operated relatively independent of each other, so there weren't many opportunities to integrate customer data across channels. Once Patagonia studied this data, it found catalog customers who were within blocks of one of its retail stores. It gave these customers reasons to visit the store to build a deeper connection with the company. This also meant Patagonia had to redefine the return on investment since these four channels were no longer unconnected silos and now supported the whole marketing mission.

Step 3: Refocus communications from the transaction to the relationship. In the era of the Internet, there's less pressure on the catalog to be the primary method of spreading the message. This also means a company can look at ways to reduce the size of its catalog, which is a socially responsible thing to do. As mentioned before, the Patagonia Web site has an authentic voice and is focused on creating a relationship. The home page has as many links to information on the company's environmental initiatives as it does commercial links to its store pages. Its press section doesn't harp on sales records or product announcements but is more focused on what Patagonia is doing for the community. At the core of this marketing strategy is the belief that its Web site is a conversation between company and customer. Patagonia is so focused on making sure its Web site is an effective tool for building community that it occasionally pulls customers out of its retail stores, sits them down in front of a computer, and gives them a gift certificate. Then these customers shop online and use the Web site while Patagonia watches and records their comments as valuable information. This very personal, in-depth approach to getting inside its customers' heads has helped Patagonia create one of the most successful socially responsible retail Web sites.[10]

Don't despair if your company hasn't yet built a business model that's as customer empowering as Patagonia's. It's a beacon in the socially responsible community, but there's no reason you can't start using some of its best practices to help create a powerful community that supports what you do.

Core Applications

To successfully build a community, you need to engage three different groups:

1. Empower your employees as messengers.
2. Empower your customers as messengers.
3. Empower your strategic partners as messengers.

Empower Your Employees as Messengers

Many tech companies from Google to Microsoft have created a new title and position in their ranks—the customer evangelist. The role of these evangelists is to engage in an ongoing dialogue with their most important customers about how the company can serve them better and how they as customers can spread the word. Recognizing that it costs five times more to acquire a customer than it does to keep a customer, this approach to marketing just makes good financial sense. Today, companies aren't just focused on branding, they're focused on bonding with their customers as well.

Ben McConnell, coauthor of *Creating Customer Evangelists,* says, "If word of mouth is the skeleton, then customer evangelism is the soul." He and his wife, coauthor Jackie Huba, cite an example of O'Reilly Publishing, a technical book publisher that created the O'Reilly Evangelist Program with a marketing employee, Simone Paddock, taking the lead in identifying customers who were already evangelists (by gathering names from other employees or doing a Google search to see what customers were saying about O'Reilly's books). Simone invited these loyal customers to help design this program, especially with respect to how the bloggers could spread the news. She asked them what they needed and found out that these evangelist bloggers wanted galley copies of the books, early copies, and they wanted to go to the O'Reilly conferences so they could report on them. Simone set all that up and created a newsletter exclusively for this group of customer evangelists.[11]

Do you have to go to the expense of hiring a customer evangelist for your company? Not necessarily. You just need to make sure your line-level employees are empowered to be advocates for your product. Not long ago, Bank of America learned that online banking customers are 11 percent more satisfied, 20 percent more likely to purchase additional products and services, and 34 percent more likely to recommend their bank's Web site. So Bank of America did everything it could to make sure their employees used the bank's online services, and now 90 percent of Bank of America employees use the Internet banking channel. The bank cites this as a major reason that 70 percent of Bank of America's new customers sign up for online banking, a higher percentage than national averages. By using the channel themselves, the tellers and call center agents become the messengers.[12]

What steps can you take to help your employees become evangelizing messengers? First and foremost, make sure your employees are not just excited about your product; make sure they're happy in their jobs. If you don't do regular work climate surveys of your employees, you will have no benchmark to understand whether their job satisfaction (and enthusiasm about your product) is growing or declining over time.

Next, make sure you have great internal communications about what's going on in the company. Are employees in the loop on new products being introduced? Are they made aware of articles written about the company (as this is often how your new customers are introduced to your company)? Do they have an ability to give real-time feedback about what they're hearing from customers about your product? Look for ways that you can regularly educate and excite your employees about your company and its products. You can't just leave this up to your customer evangelists or salespeople.

Create a dialogue with your employees about the importance of customer word of mouth. Ask them about experiences they've had as customers that led to positive or negative word of mouth, and delve deeper into their perception of your customers' current satisfaction with your product. In fact, consider reviewing your customer satisfaction data with the line-level employees and get their opinions on what you're hearing from customers. It's amazing how few companies regularly present this data to the employees who have the most influence on improving these scores.

Talk about how employees can identify potential evangelizing customers and how they can pass these names on to their managers or the marketing department so the company can strike up a deeper relationship with these potential customer evangelists. Create a contest and give a prize to the line-level employee who identifies the most evangelists in the month. Your employees' word of mouth about your company to friends and family is important, but, even more so, the way they build a relationship with your customers goes a long way to determining whether your customers become part of your cheerleading squad.

Empower Your Customers as Messengers

Soon after nineteen-year-old Mo Siegel started Celestial Seasonings herbal tea company in 1969, he realized that as a small business he needed to encourage his customers to tell their friends about this product, as Celestial Seasonings didn't have the budget to do any significant advertising. Mo enclosed a note in each box of tea that asked people to serve this tea to their friends and to spread the word. This homespun approach to empowering word of mouth paid off big-time, as the early buzz on

Celestial Seasonings was that it was an alternative to the old-time tea companies like Lipton.[13]

More recently, Clif Bar chose to engage with its customers in another unique approach to product packaging. Given its Luna bar was tailor-made for women, the Clif team created a Luna dedication that would appear on the back of each Luna bar. The company reached out to its customers asking them for personal dedications to women who have touched their lives in a meaningful way. Yana Kushner, director of Luna equity and advanced product development, explains, "By giving them a piece of ourselves, they feel part of the Luna family. It's a two-way street. It keeps them excited and passionate, and it also keeps us internally passionate."[14]

This idea was so popular that they couldn't print all of the dedications on the Luna bars. They can now be found in three places: on the Luna wrapper, on the online dedications quilt, and on the handmade quilt that travels around the country to the various Luna events (like the Lunafest film festival).

Mainstream companies have jumped on this bandwagon, realizing that customers listen to other customers more than they do to the company. Ban Deodorant encouraged young women to create simple minimovies and post them on the Ban Web site. These homegrown movies or ads, which feature titles like *Ban Drama* or *Ban Peer Pressure,* were created by young customers who are speaking to the emotional challenges facing young women. The *Wall Street Journal* reported that Ban's new approach led to annual sales growth of nearly 14 percent after three years of decline.[15]

But beware of the risks associated with empowering your customers. First, the more you choreograph your customers, the more your customers may feel manipulated. It's one thing for a company to toot its own horn, but when the company treats its customer like a ventriloquist's dummy, you risk losing trust.

Second, if you want to empower your customers, you'd better feel pretty confident about your product quality—because true empowerment (as in an open source blog on your Web site that allows customers to comment on the company or product) means that you'll hear the good, the bad, and the ugly. Finally, be cautious about using financial incentives to encourage customers to spread the word. When you realize a friend was, in essence, bribed to sign you up as a customer, it won't just hurt the company's credibility—it also could ruin the friendship.

Empower Your Strategic Partners as Messengers

Many companies have strategic partners—be they affiliated marketing organizations, nonprofits that have a philanthropic connection, or supplier organizations—that can help get the message out.

When Joie de Vivre Hospitality launched the literary-inspired Hotel Rex in San Francisco in the mid-1990s, it was a difficult time for arts organizations across the country. The National Endowment for the Arts (NEA) was coming under heavy political pressure from conservatives due to their concerns about the morality of some of the art the NEA was funding. Additionally, many were questioning whether the federal government should be subsidizing the arts when that could better be left to nonprofit organizations. The net result was that many San Francisco arts organizations were in financial jeopardy because of the potential funding cutbacks.

Chip made a decision to engage his arts-minded guests at the new Hotel Rex to help support the local arts community. Since Joie de Vivre had the credibility of being an arts-supporting company for many years, he was able to build a strategic relationship with twelve arts organizations. The primary purpose was to support the arts by allowing hotel guests to donate a portion of their stay to any of these groups—the dual benefit was to expand the hotel's reach to a perfectly matched customer.

This Patron of the Arts program not only made the hotel guest feel good (and led to valuable word of mouth), but also allowed Hotel Rex to tap into the mailing lists of these twelve beneficiary organizations. Since it was in the best interests of these arts organizations to encourage their supporters to stay in the hotel, or have their friends or associates stay in the hotel, Hotel Rex was able to do significant direct mail marketing to these arts cheerleaders. This was an inexpensive way for the Rex to build its community upon its launch, and it was also a targeted means of connecting with the kind of hotel guests who would appreciate the cultured and sophisticated nature of the Hotel Rex product.

You may have existing strategic partners or you may not. The key features of a great strategic marketing partnership are a common demographic or psychographic community between the two organizations, an offer that provides a synergistic benefit to the community members, and parallel goals that create mutual benefit to the two organizations.

NEW SEASONS MARKET

EMPOWERING PEOPLE AS MESSENGERS

As we've said in this chapter, storytelling is much more compelling than pure statistics. New Seasons Market has employed storytelling to great success as a part of its ethos and culture, and it is one of the most powerful tools in its marketing approach. In particular, New Seasons has empowered its employees to be great storytellers, messengers, and ambassadors for its brand. The stories that staff tell, the relationships they build, and the communication they have with customers very quickly creates real engagement between customers and the New Seasons experience. These relationships ultimately foster a sense of personal identification and community among New Seasons' customers.

Employees are trained and encouraged to talk with customers and to be ambassadors of the brand. At new employee training, the CEO and the president spend a half day with new staff. Brian Rohter describes the training's core message: "We tell them that every single staff member, from the sixteen-year-old courtesy clerk to the president of the company, not only has the same authority to make customers happy, but has the same responsibility to do so."[16] Situations are established throughout the shopping experience that provide ample opportunities for these interactions to occur in ways that are radically different from a typical supermarket shopping experience. Employees are hired as experts in the areas in which they work. Many employees come to New Seasons with strong expertise in food and wine. Numerous chefs, cooks, and other foodies work at New Seasons. In fact, every store has an in-store chef, whose job includes talking with customers and other store staff about the cooking and food needs of customers. In addition to the in-store chef, many of the employees behind the meat counter are culinary-institute-trained chefs, who give advice, recipes, and assistance to customers.

In-store nutritionists set free appointments with customers to design a diet for their health needs and to take them on a personalized store tour. The nutritionists are also available for customers to just drop in and ask questions. The Solutions Counter at the front of every store offers samples of delicious products (a great conversation starter) and is in a highly visible location where the main purpose is to help customers find solutions by talking with staff (again, a major contrast with the old-fashioned, reflective glass supermarket store office).

All staff members are given a "get out of jail free" card, which allows them to leave what they are doing in their assigned area if they see that a customer needs help or if they notice a situation where someone needs to find a solution. Instead of passing the customer off to someone else, they can take care of it themselves and make sure that the customer gets what he or she needs. Employees are powerful brand messengers, partly because they are hired with this role in mind but also because they are provided training and tools, and they work in an environment designed to encourage conversation with customers. Primarily, they are effective brand ambassadors and messengers because they truly experience the brand promise themselves. New Seasons empowers employees and treats them as well as they want their employees to treat the customers. As a result, employees are able to be authentic and enthusiastic representatives of the company.

From relationships that employees build and the stories they share, many New Seasons customers become engaged stakeholders who themselves are messengers. Customers have nominated the company for community awards, posted positive Internet blog entries that use New Seasons as an example, and have created an incredible word-of-mouth network about New Seasons being the place to go for great food and great community. For New Seasons Market, people are the most powerful messengers.[17]

Empower Your Community

Whether it's you, your colleagues, staff, investors, customers, or the media, every person who comes into contact with your business is a potential storyteller for your brand. It's one thing to hear people talk about a great product—it is an eye and mind opener to hear someone share a love affair they're having with a company and/or how they feel about belonging to a real community. This is the Holy Grail for any company. And socially responsible companies have an advantage in creating this level of relationship based upon their values proposition.

Now let's explore what it means to walk the talk and why authenticity and transparency are paramount to any socially responsible endeavor.

Walk the talk

PRACTICE 9: BE AUTHENTIC AND TRANSPARENT

Today's customers have good reason to be skeptical. The marketplace is filled with products that don't work; businesses flood media with campaigns to improve their image without the good business practices to back them up; and politicians and governments at every level appear to be distorting the truth in alarming ways. Trust is at an all-time low. More than ever, customers are demanding integrity from their chosen brands, and as a socially responsible business, you are uniquely positioned to capture these customers as your own. Why? Because you walk the talk. It has never been more critical that your words and actions reflect your core values. In this chapter, we will focus on authenticity and transparency. We think of authenticity as the foundation upon which the marketing program for a business is built and transparency as the insurance policy that creates trust and drives accountability.

Jeffrey Hollender, CEO of Seventh Generation, decided to identify and disclose all of the ingredients used in Seventh Generation's products even though disclosure is not required by any regulation. By taking this action, Hollender was providing information to his customers that would help them make informed choices, and he was demonstrating authenticity and transparency. As a green brand that responds to customers' desire to tread lightly on the planet, Seventh Generation established important trust by demonstrating that it would make only authentic claims for its products. When products contain ingredients that are not sustainably produced, it says so. In essence, Seventh Generation is telling its customers, "While we have removed many harmful substances compared to conventional brands, we too must make products that work, and we are still striving to find alternatives."[1] In addition, Seventh Generation posts this information on its Web site, further demonstrating that it will make only authentic claims and is committed to operating its business transparently.

Values-based customers have a finely tuned "BS meter" and a deep desire to authenticate the claims made by the companies that they support. While the loyalty of values-based customers is deeply desirable, their wrath, if they discover false claims, is formidable. Some marketers have characterized the values-based customer as an information hound. These customers desire the ability to garner detailed information. They often serve as a brand's most valuable distribution channel for information as they discover it. They pass along details that either reinforce the brand with others or call the brand into question.

In chapter 7, we cautioned you not to leave out the emotional content and links to values that are essential to customer decision making in favor of data alone. That remains true, but in order to create an authentic experience for your customers, and demonstrate transparency, you must provide ways for these customers to discover the information to justify their belief in your claims. Access to this information, and evidence of your commitment to behave authentically and transparently, is critical to establishing trust and long-term customer relationships.

Beyond the true believer audience, the broader base of customers also holds the desire for authentic experiences with the products and services they encounter. They want the ability to validate their trust through access to real information. They too want transparency.

When your company looks at creating marketing strategies that convey authenticity and transparency, it is important that you are doing it for the right reasons. In other words, your choices to strive for a socially responsible workplace, a socially responsible supply chain, and a relationship of trust with your customers and your community should be based upon the desire to meet multiple bottom lines. Don't make these choices as a means to the end of creating positive imaging. It is important for socially responsible businesses to *show* more than to *tell*.

Customers who have the opportunity to experience and discover the authenticity of your product, service, and brand claims, will establish relationships of trust with your brand. They are likely to become messengers of your socially responsible positioning. Remember the power of people as messengers from chapter 8? Well, delivering authentic experiences and providing your customers with information through your own transparency creates third-party messengers for your brand. Their authentic experience with your company, and the stories they can tell, create the most powerful means of conveying the good social, environmental, and business choices of your organization.

Core Applications

To help you build authenticity and transparency into your own marketing efforts, we have identified five applications you can use to integrate this practice into your business. They include

1. Do the right thing.
2. Live the brand *inside* your organization.
3. Expose yourself.
4. Let customers have an authentic experience.
5. Make marketing choices that mesh with your values.

Do the Right Thing

No business is perfect. Another way you can assure authenticity and appropriately market your social responsibility is to make changes in operations and procedures that address unsustainable practices and improve your social impacts. When you make the choice to do the right thing, you create additional opportunities for customers, suppliers, employees, and partners to experience the authenticity of your brand claim.

One example of a very large multinational company making such a change is Chiquita's move into organic banana production. Chiquita is one of the largest banana producers in the world, growing about 25 percent of the bananas sold in the United States and Europe. It realized that the market was changing and that its customers increasingly wanted healthy organic food. It also recognized that its customers and stakeholders were aware and concerned about the environmental and social impacts of banana growing. So Chiquita made the decision to move to production of organically certified bananas.

To ensure it could make an authentic claim, Chiquita entered into a collaboration with Rainforest Alliance, an independent nongovernmental organization (NGO), to establish certification standards and to conduct annual independent inspections of all of Chiquita's banana farms. The independent inspections hold Chiquita accountable to be in compliance with Rainforest Alliance's environmental and social standards. Rainforest Alliance has certified all of Chiquita's company-owned farms in Latin America. In addition, many of the independent farms that supply Chiquita with bananas are becoming certified, thereby increasing both the acreage and the population working in the banana industry that benefit from Rainforest Alliance's strict standards. Chiquita has also certified all of the company's farms to the rigid international social standards of ISO 14000 (a global series of environmental management system standards) and Social Accountability International SA8000 criteria (the most rigorous international standard for humane workplaces).

The environmental, social, and economic impacts of Chiquita's decision to go organic are massive, considering the company's significant market share, distribution, and marketing reach. Chiquita has made a significant operations change that has begun to improve its corporate image and has created a new value/values proposition for its lead product. Chiquita has also seen an excellent return on investment. According to the Rainforest Alliance, "Although Chiquita has invested more than $20 million to make required capital improvements, the company has reduced its production costs by more than $100 million."[2]

Important to the point we are making about transparency is the choice that Chiquita made to collaborate with the Rainforest Alliance. Its commitment to use an established NGO, rather than create an industry-managed group, meant that a credible and truly independent organization was establishing the standards, conducting the certification, and monitoring Chiquita's ongoing compliance. Both Chiquita and the Rainforest Alliance post information about the certification program on their Web sites. Chiquita's corporate social responsibility report provides detailed information on the process it has gone through, including its challenges and successes. Chiquita's choice to make its operations transparent for an outside organization (and therefore its customers and the marketplace) authenticated its claims, created trusted messengers, and provided the ability for advocacy groups and customers to hold Chiquita accountable. Chiquita's leadership readily acknowledges the value of the partnership.

"In addition to gaining improved morale and productivity in our farms, we have saved money in the process. Everybody wins—the workers, the company and the environment, not to mention the Rainforest Alliance, which deserves enormous credit for showing us a better way," said Bob Kistinger, president and chief operating officer of the Chiquita Fresh Group.[3]

It is never the wrong time to do the right thing. Make sure you recognize your own areas for improvement and that you step up to address these challenges. Also, be willing to make changes that take advantage of new opportunities, changes in the marketplace, or new insights that can help your company walk the talk.

Live the Brand Inside Your Organization

Throughout this book we have emphasized the fact that your customers' experience is significantly influenced by the culture of your company. The way in which you operate internally—how your employees, suppliers, shareholders, and stakeholders are treated—has a great influence on how the market will experience you. In other words, how you work on the inside has a great impact on how you look on the outside. It is far easier to build relationships of trust with customers when employees are happy and believe in the company. It is nearly impossible to create belief in a company's socially responsible position if the employees don't believe it and live it for themselves.

Many socially responsible companies do align their human resource policies, staff training programs, and purchasing to their values. A few brief examples include gDiapers, ShoreBank, and Norm Thompson.

gDiapers has staked a claim on being a company that is family and earth friendly. It decided from day one that its business model needed to support a workplace that keeps parents connected with their kids and makes life easier for working parents. gDiapers established on-site day care and closes the office each day at 4:30 so that parents and kids get home with plenty of time for dinner, baths, reading, and quality family time. And it provides four weeks paid leave for all employees.[4]

ShoreBank conducts an annual confidential all-employee satisfaction survey and shares the results with every employee. It celebrates the areas where it excels and where it has improved, and it openly commits to addressing the areas of concern.[5]

Norm Thompson, a catalog company, combined the position of director of communications and that of corporate responsibility director to make sure its values are in alignment inside and outside the organization.[6]

Examine the core value claims that your company makes to customers and to the community. Are you living up to the same claims inside your organization? Make sure that your personnel policies, company culture, and purchasing practices align with your values. If you don't already do so, consider giving your employees a confidential satisfaction survey that includes questions about how they experience your company's values and if they recommend the company to others as potential customers or employees. Take action based upon the results. When you live your brand inside the organization, it will be better communicated to the outside.

Expose Yourself

Like Seventh Generation, many socially responsible businesses may have aspects of their operations, products, and services that are not pristine or utopian. Though Seventh Generation has a strong desire to develop cleaning products that are free of toxic substances, it also knows that it must create products that clean people's houses.[7] While all socially responsible businesses strive to do better, few, if any, claim to be totally socially responsible. Making the choice to expose yourself, make honest claims, and disclose your challenges helps authenticate the honest motivation behind your values proposition. This self-disclosure can also insure you against customer misperceptions and unrealistic expectations that lead to disappointment.

For example, New Seasons Market has a strong commitment to supporting sustainable food production and makes very public claims about its desire to do so. At the same time, it sells a wide variety of products to meet its customers' needs and desires. New Seasons discloses information on the country of origin, whether food is organic, and even which seafood is from sustainable or endangered fisheries. Customers are immediately able to see what in the store is sustainable and what is not. While New Seasons has a goal of carrying and supporting primarily sustainable products, it also recognizes that its core value proposition is to serve as the ultimate neighborhood grocery and be the place where customers can do all of their weekly shopping. By being transparent with what it carries in the store, New Seasons Market assures the authenticity of its claims and helps customers make informed purchases.[8]

A better-known example of the importance of transparency is Nike's management of its international supply chain. After advocacy groups mobilized pressure on Nike to change and become more transparent, Nike acknowledged that it needed to be more vigilant in monitoring work conditions in the overseas factories where its products are made. It has engaged in a focused effort to increase transparency. Nike has launched its Transparency 101 Program, which is designed to create public awareness of the company's activities, including the monitoring of factories where it operates, and ensure that the practices in each country are in compliance with Nike's Code of Conduct.[9] Its engagement with the Natural Step Framework (an international set of scientifically valid principles for sustainability that address environmental and social impacts)[10] and its endorsement of the CERES Principles (a set of international environmental, social, and transparent corporate governance principles developed by the independent Coalition for Environmentally Responsible Economies) are additional steps Nike has taken to provide transparency and accountability around its social and environmental commitments.[11]

By being honest and open, you can address issues, mitigate criticism, and build credibility for your value and values claims. Share your decision-making processes, your product ingredients, your supply chain information, and other information that authenticates your claims. Tell your employees, customers, and stakeholders what actions you are taking in areas that need improvement by using the communication tools you control. Your Web site, printed material, product packaging, and business locations can all tell the story of your authentic actions. Transparency allows you to get caught doing the right thing.

Let Customers Have an Authentic Experience

Even as technology has created great advancements, it has also created more complexity and, in some ways, less opportunity for personal relationships and connection. Our sense of community, place, and opportunities to have truly unique experiences seem increasingly challenged by mass merchandising, corporate consolidation, globalization, and an increasingly homogenous commercial experience.

Both of us travel extensively for business and often feel like we have entered the twilight zone—in city after city, we see the exact same stores, generally in the same proximity to each other. Cable and satellite television offer hundreds of channels, yet the consolidation of media has actually narrowed the content, diversity of programming, and news coverage. At the same time, people's need and desire for community has not diminished. Therein exists an opportunity. While all businesses can benefit by meeting this need through creating authentic experiences, socially responsible businesses have a distinct advantage.

By their nature, socially responsible businesses are grounded in creating authentic experiences. Restaurants like the White Dog Cafe (a popular Philadelphia eatery that has been a leader in the use of organic and sustainable agriculture and whose owner, Judy Wicks, is a national leader in the socially responsible business community) connects customers to place by using foods that are fresh from local farms (much from Lancaster County). Judy describes how the White Dog Cafe connects local sourcing and its commitment to service: "A hallmark of the restaurant is buying most of our food from local organic and humane farmers. In this way we serve our customers with healthy food, our community by supporting local family farmers, and nature by supporting organics and humane, pasture-raised meat and poultry."[12] Chip's restaurant Millennium creates unique food experiences that are about people (the chefs and staff) and place (the food of the region and the culinary style of the culture).

Independent media such as Link TV and *Utne* magazine provide audiences with provocative and alternative news, information, and entertainment. Joie de Vivre's online "Yvette the Hotel Matchmaker" program connects customers with "off the beaten path" activities that will interest them and matches the customer with local residents who volunteer to show visitors their San Francisco. Producer-retailers like Hanna Andersson (kids' clothing) and Rejuvenation (light fixture and hardware manufacturer and retailer) offer products of long-lasting quality and reduce unnecessary new purchases. Working Assets turns your long distance and wireless service into a communication tool to advance your values, while ShoreBank turns your FDIC-insured certificate of deposit into an investment in neighborhood revitalization. Put your authentic experience out front and ask these questions:

- Question anonymity—Give customers the opportunity to see the unique "fingerprints" of the people who have designed, created, and delivered its products and services. Kettle Foods, which manufactures Kettle potato chips and a variety of nut butters, has a deep commitment to natural and organic foods and a brand that is centered on the craft of creating its foods. Visit its Web site and click on "Committed People" to put names and faces on quality assurance managers and line staff, and click on "What We Stand For" to get inside the process from selecting farm fresh potatoes to hand cooking small batches of chips. By connecting to people and demystifying the process, Kettle's brand transforms a commodity into a handcrafted product that builds relationships with customers.[13]

- Question the value of sameness—As we discussed in chapter 4, each of Chip's hotels in the Joie de Vivre family has been designed around a set of aspirational descriptors to provide the customer with an authentic experience of identity refreshment. Rather than each hotel having a Joie de Vivre hotel chain feel, the unifying characteristic is the diversity of experiences among the hotels and the authentic experience for each hotel guest, ranging from the embodiment of *Rolling Stone* magazine to the *New Yorker*.

- Question rigid formulas and criteria for decisions—Shore-Bank's loan officers don't just look at the financial numbers, plug them into a formula, and approve or deny a real estate loan. Rather, they get to know the customer and the project. They can help customers walk away from a bad deal, get training and technical assistance to help them qualify, and identify and fund additional renovations to make the project more energy efficient.[14]

Don't shy away from what is authentic about your company. Make it easy for customers to have a real experience, and they will tell the story.

Make Marketing Choices That Mesh with Your Values

Your company's marketing materials—from your advertising to the media stories you pitch and the imagery on your Web site— are all reflections of your brand. They can either ring true to the values of your company or create contradictions between your principles and the experience the marketplace has of your organization. We have advocated that socially responsible marketing and communication need not be humorless, sterile, fact-laden, or limited to the price and product offer. But we want to be clear that the execution of your marketing plan must support your core values.

Do the choices you make about the imagery, the casting, the copywriting, and the placement of advertising mesh with your company's diversity and social justice values? Do the choices you make about the design, paper, printing process, and distribution strategy for your print collateral mesh with your company's environmental values? Does your Web site content convey only product and service information? Or does your Web site also provide opportunities for customers to give feedback, have access to in-depth information that supports your product and brand claims, and connect to your social causes and relevant social issues? There is no one right answer. But as a business leader, you should ask yourself the questions. And the answers should align with your company's values.

A Few Questions to Ask
When Designing Marketing Tools

Reduce resource use through the design process by asking these questions:

- Is a printed piece even necessary? If so, what size does it need to be? Have you designed it to use paper as efficiently as possible? (Ask your designer and printer about fitting the maximum number on the parent sheet to minimize waste.) What size will optimize printing on the parent sheet? Have you determined the distribution strategy in advance so you can print the right quantity rather than the "safe" quantity? (Avoid the twenty cases of brochures in the storeroom syndrome.) Have you designed the piece so it has more than one use for your company or for the end user? Have you designed the piece to be easily recyclable (no metal or plastic fasteners, windows, etc.)?

- Have you specified use of paper with the maximum postconsumer waste recycled content possible?

- Have you sought out FSC-certified printers that use less-toxic inks, have excellent air quality safeguards, and control water and energy use?

- Is your "creative" in line with your values and the values of your customers? Have you looked at your casting choices, image selection, and copy to assure it walks your talk and is in alignment with your mission?

- Have you made it easy for customers to find additional information and details that back your claims and provide transparency?

- Have you provided opportunities for your customers and other community members to provide you with feedback on your Web site?

- Is your Web site compliant with Section 6 of the Americans with Disabilities Act (which makes sure your Web site is accessible for persons with disabilities)?[15]

Here are a few examples of companies that have designed their marketing execution to mesh with their values.

Women's clothing designer Eileen Fisher's print advertising has featured both models and company employees—women with whom her customers can readily identify. Her marketing features women of all ages who look like professionals, artists, mothers, neighbors, community leaders, and thousands of other real people rather than runway supermodels. Her advertising still connects with emotion by conveying beauty, sans stereotypes.[16] The beauty cleansing brand Dove also found great success with its Campaign for Real Beauty that used real women—not models—who were shaped like the majority of women as opposed to the often emaciated models seen in fashion magazines.

ShoreBank has diversified the images and testimonials from customers on its Web site. Advertising and marketing materials accurately convey its diverse customer mix and its appeal to a broad customer base. It has also put into place guidelines for materials that specify environmentally sustainable design and printing practices.[17]

Flexcar's tagline is "The smart way to have a car." This connects environmentally oriented customers with the reality-based need that many people have—to reduce its environmental impact while also having the ability to pick up a piece of furniture at the swap meet or go on the occasional weekend road trip. Its tagline honestly connects with the primary customer decision driver (transportation need) and creates guilt-free permission for its green customers.[18]

Rejuvenation's catalog features real stories from customers and profiles of the workers that manufacture the light fixtures, highlighting both the use of the product and the craftsmanship, integrity, and fair workplace conditions that go into creating its lights.[19]

We encourage you to make choices that reflect your values when you select marketing strategies and throughout the process of concept development, design, writing, and production of your marketing tactics. If you do, you will be effective in your marketing and back up your authentic socially responsible commitments.

BE AUTHENTIC AND TRANSPARENT

One of New Seasons Market's core brand claims is being truly local—locally owned, locally operated, and deeply committed to supporting the regional food economy. It strives to create a strong connection between rural producers and urban customers. As part of demonstrating authenticity around its claim of supporting the regional food economy and local producers, New Seasons has led the industry in labeling fresh food with its geographic origin (not only country of origin, but state, region, and, where possible, the actual farm). New Seasons provides this information on product labels, price signs, and in the informational brochures and signs at its produce area, meat counter, dairy case, and prepared food and deli areas. "We look at our 100,000 customers as part of our community and caretakers of our mission," explains Brian Rohter. "When we open ourselves up, share information, and admit we can make mistakes they tell us to correct, it is very powerful."[20]

New Seasons firmly believes that customers armed with information will be able to make choices to support the local economy. It feels compelled to consistently make its local commitment transparent to its suppliers and customers.

As we discussed in earlier chapters, New Seasons has instituted many programs to increase the amount of locally grown and produced products that are carried in its stores.

New Seasons establishes long-term relationships with ranching families, farm families, family-owned fishing vessels, and regional food processors. To make this commitment even more transparent, it developed its Home Grown program. New Seasons defined its local food shed as being the entire eco-region of Oregon, Washington, and Northern California. In addition to providing fresh food from the farm, ranch, and ocean, New Seasons also wanted to make sure that it was stocking prepared foods, canned foods, and nonfood products from the same Home Grown region. It identified everything it sold that was produced in the Home Grown region from canned pie filling to greeting cards and gift items. New Seasons created a Home Grown logo and put it on all of the pricing signs for fresh food products. It also created a color-coded shelf-tag system so that the pricing on the grocery shelves in the middle of the store (where the nonperishable items and frozen foods are stocked) indicates to shoppers that an item is grown, produced, or both in the Home Grown food shed. Large display signs at the entrance of each store introduce shoppers to the Home Grown program and invite customers to look for the Home Grown logo and the yellow shelf tags.

Just as the Home Grown program has created transparency about what products at New Seasons are local, it has also created transparency about what products are not. With this clear visual indicator of its commitment and the distance the product needed to travel to get to the market, New Seasons is able to make a legitimate claim to its customers about its commitment to the local food economy. It is able to focus attention on adding local products to the mix and bit by bit to increase the percentage of yellow Home Grown labels in the store. When it comes to its commitment to the local food economy to provide honest information to its customers, New Seasons Market walks the talk.[21]

Walk the Talk

Ultimately, socially responsible business operations can enhance a company's marketing efforts and help maintain relationships of trust with diverse stakeholders. Being authentic to your values and utilizing transparency are practices that will hold you accountable and differentiate your marketing. Remember that transparency is an important marketing strategy because it provides your customers and other stakeholders with the opportunity to validate your company's claims, have a greater sense of ownership, and serve as third-party endorsers and messengers. Whether your company is making business changes that improve operating practices, investing in your internal culture, disclosing the gaps in your claims, creating authentic experiences for customers, or designing marketing tools to reflect your values, walking the talk is at the heart of true relationship marketing.

Finally, let's look at how you can use your voice to change the world.

Use the power of your voice to change the world

**PRACTICE 10: LEVERAGE MARKETING
FOR SOCIAL IMPACT**

Many of the socially responsible business leaders we talk to started their companies with a desire to change the world. Some wanted to use the power of business to impact customers, employees, and communities. Others were escaping an existence in the single bottom line corporate world that had left them saying, "There has to be a better way." And still others were motivated by a little bit of both. The founders of ShoreBank are one such example.

This visionary financial institution was started by four bankers who in 1973 could no longer stomach a standard banking practice of the day called redlining (excluding entire neighborhoods from access to loans based upon their race and income). They didn't buy the conventional wisdom that defined certain communities as unbankable. So with the help of a handful of mission-driven investors, they bought a bank on the south side of Chicago and proved that a bank could make a difference *and* a profit. In doing so, they helped create the community development banking industry.[1]

Whether a socially responsible business starts out intending to change a community or the world—or just to create a fair workplace—the opportunity to leverage its voice and marketing power is one reason so many socially responsible business leaders see themselves as social entrepreneurs. This final chapter explores using the power of your business to influence and impact the world around you. While this power of business is not new (just think back to the influence of business from railroad and steel barons to the oil and automobile industries), the use of business voice to advance a more just and sustainable world is now being pioneered by socially responsible businesses.

Remember, choosing how and when to use business voice to advance a cause and create social impact is different for every business. The point we want to make is not that every socially responsible business must walk in lockstep, be politically oriented, support a preapproved set of causes, or focus its marketing program on social change. Rather, our point is to make sure that as business owners and managers who are striving for more social responsibility, you are aware of the power of your business's voice and that you can make conscious decisions about when and how to use it.

Let's take a look at why we believe your marketing infrastructure, or business voice, can be such a powerful force. While many don't stop to think of their own businesses in this context, we readily see business—particularly the marketing footprint—as having a potentially incredible reach. From the influence of corporate media—where a handful of companies control over 80 percent of America's prime-time news and own the top twenty news Web sites—to the omnipresent awareness of global brands like Coke, McDonald's, and Microsoft, the power of business to shape opinion, mold consumer trends, define markets, and influence policy is no surprise.[2] Business and the platform of business marketing has become an increasingly dominant institution in our society due to three key assets that amplify business voice:

- People—Businesses have direct relationships and the commensurate opportunity for direct communication with employees, customers, strategic partners, and suppliers.

- Investment in communication tools—Businesses have numerous vehicles that are used to convey their messages, including physical locations, online presence, advertising and public relations, product packaging, and direct mail.

- Significant access to mind/time share—In today's media- and business-centered society, business is the dominant institution in many people's lives—whether or not we're always conscious of it. Just think about the time an average American spends at work, the store, the restaurant, the espresso stand, the bank, and doing other day-to-day errands, as well as online at commercial Web sites. With each visit, we are receiving messages on packages for the food we eat and the products we buy—constantly consuming print, electronic, and out of home media.

What often surprises socially responsible business leaders is the power and reach of their own brands, supply chains, employee and customer relationships, and community presence. The ability to use this power to be a force for strong, sustainable, and just communities is our tenth practice: *Leverage Marketing for Social Impact.*

Core Applications

We have identified six applications that you can use to help integrate this practice into your business. They include

1. Design your core product or service as a social change tool.
2. Empower your customers as change agents.
3. Take a stand.

4. Use cause-related marketing.
5. Put philanthropy at the center of your value/values proposition.
6. Harness the power of business-to-business purchasing.

Design Your Core Product or Service as a Social Change Tool

One of the strongest examples of socially responsible businesses using the power of voice is when companies design their core product or service to help drive social change. When ShoreBank makes a loan or accepts a mission-based deposit, it is using traditional financial services to advance its customer's community vision to reinvigorate neighborhoods and improve the environment. Customers who buy certificates of deposit from Shore-Bank are receiving the same FDIC insurance and market-rate interest they would from other banks while directing their deposits to be invested in improvement of urban neighborhoods and natural, resource-dependent, rural communities. Similarly, when an entrepreneur receives a loan from ShoreBank to rehabilitate an urban apartment building, or a small business uses a loan to expand its operations, they help create a strong community—which includes quality housing owned and managed by local residents and good local jobs in areas where many other banks would not have invested.[3]

To a great degree the entire field of socially responsible investments (SRIs) has developed as a product that puts the power of economic voice behind socially responsible causes by improving corporate accountability, environmental performance, and human rights while empowering individual and institutional investors to express their values with their investment choices. From a PAX World Funds ad that proclaims, "Pollution. We're not buying it,"[4] to Calvert's campaign that states, "Honesty is the Best Corporate Excess" and encourages investors to demand corporate accountability and transparency,[5]

SRIs invite investors to put their money where their mouth is. Beyond their advertising, the investment screening, proxy voting, and community development investments that SRIs make with their customers' assets—their basic product—drive social change. Amy Domini, founder and CEO of Domini Social Investments and one of the founders of the SRI industry, was named by *Time* magazine as one of the 100 Most Influential People of 2005.[6] Domini is deeply devoted to socially responsible investing: she literally wrote the book on the subject, *Ethical Investing*. Her efforts have spurred hundreds of companies, from the Gap to Ford to Intel, to evaluate their impact on the environment and human rights. Her influence? Helping investors with her fund—and ultimately with many other funds—impacts how business is done and in many ways changes the world. Today, a segment that started as an alternative movement holds nearly 9.4 percent of the invested assets in the United States and is growing rapidly.[7]

Look at your product and services. Do they serve to drive social change? Can you design them so they can? Do you leverage your product's impacts by influencing others in your industry?

Empower Your Customers as Change Agents

Michael Kieschnick, president, chief operating officer, and co-founder of Working Assets, is very clear that his product, his marketing, in fact his whole business is about empowering customers to change the world. He points out that his base product—wireless service—is a readily available commodity no different from that offered by his competitors. However, Working Assets' model—which empowers customers to easily advocate issues with their elected officials (through the Citizen Action program), direct a portion of the company's revenues to the causes they care about, and engage in policy issues—serves as the company's unique value proposition and a compelling values proposition.

Before Working Assets, who could imagine that reading and paying your phone bill could better connect you to the issues you care about, give you the ability to vote with your pocketbook every time you make a call, and radically simplify telling your elected officials what you think—by virtue of a free long distance call? Working Assets has amplified the power of its customers' voices.[8]

Stonyfield Farm looked at its yogurt container lids as an untapped opportunity to empower its customers to help advance a more sustainable environment. Through Stonyfield's Lid Program, the company puts messages about the environment and sustainable agriculture on every lid, educating its customers and often giving them the opportunity to impact the issue via the Web.[9]

Consider using your packaging, billing, in-store signs, and other communications vehicles to provide customers with opportunities to directly impact issues. By doing so, you can use the power of your business's voice to help customers positively impact their communities and the world.

Take a Stand

As we touched on at the beginning of this chapter, business often uses the considerable power of its voice to take a stand on issues. In many cases, businesses have used voice in ways that many of us would see as irresponsible. In fact, when we think of companies taking a stand, we usually think of industry-funded campaigns or individual company-sponsored ads, in which business voice has been used to fight health-care reform, limit tougher air and water quality standards, fight living wage laws, oppose country-of-origin food labeling, or limit liability for products such as guns and tobacco. But taking a stand is not limited to protecting the status quo or the interests of big business. Socially responsible businesses can also use their voices to take a stand.

Self-Help credit union, based in Durham, North Carolina, became gravely concerned about the continuing and pervasive practice of predatory lending, which charges higher interest rates and higher financing fees to low-income applicants. Self-Help decided to take a stand. It created the affiliated Center for Responsible Lending (CRL), a national nonprofit dedicated to protecting home ownership and family wealth by working to eliminate abusive financial practices. CRL has provided technical assistance in more than twenty states and on Capitol Hill to advance legislation that protects both borrowers and the marketplace.[10]

Well known for rugged boot wear, Timberland has produced themed ad campaigns, provided in-store information, and funded human rights groups to fight bigotry and discrimination. One print ad campaign featured a headline calling on customers to "Give Racism the Boot." Through its Code of Conduct program, Timberland works to ensure that its products are made in workplaces that are fair, safe, and nondiscriminatory. Timberland also partners with and funds human rights groups, nongovernmental organizations, and international agencies, such as Verité, CARE, and Social Accountability International, to develop programs focused on continuous improvement in human rights.[11]

Clif Bar publicly supported introduction of the Precautionary Principle (a San Francisco ordinance to require proving that chemicals are safe prior to using them in products rather than waiting until they are proven toxic to people).[12]

Norm Thompson pushed against the industry norm of not using recycled content in catalogs by testing batches of catalogs with various percentages of recycled content and sharing their results with the executives of other catalog companies. It presented its case, and what many would consider proprietary findings, at industry conferences to encourage other companies to follow its lead.[13]

In Eric's home state of Oregon, it was legal to discriminate in employment based upon a person's sexual orientation. Over three hundred businesses joined forces and created the Fair Workplace Project, adding nondiscrimination protections to their employment policies and being listed as Fair Workplace signatories. This voluntary effort of employers taking a stand means that thousands of Oregon workers are now safe from being fired or discriminated against due to their sexual orientation.[14]

Whether you are communicating with your customers and employees; testifying before city councils, legislators, and congressional committees; demanding responsible practices from your suppliers; or using your influence with your industry and trade associations—your company provides many platforms from which to take a stand.

Use Cause-Related Marketing

Connecting your company or products to a cause can amplify the voice of a community need through the reach of your marketing. For instance, consider the nation's breast cancer epidemic. In 2005, over 40,000 women died of breast cancer and more than 200,000 new cases of invasive breast cancer were expected to be diagnosed.[15] Many of these women do not smoke or have a genetic predisposition to cancer. An increasing body of evidence has linked environmental causes (the presence of known and suspected poisons in cosmetics, the presence of known toxins in groundwater, toxins in the built environment, and other exposures to toxins) to breast and other cancers.

With the prevailing public attention to breast cancer focused on raising awareness about mammograms and the need to fund research for a cure, this important factor that impacts people's health was not garnering the attention it warrants. The Breast Cancer Fund, a national nonprofit dedicated to eliminating the environmental causes of breast cancer, has found a powerful ally to get the word out through its cause-related partnership with Luna bar. Beyond the financial contribution to the Breast Cancer Fund's work, Luna raises awareness of the issue through its Lunafest film series, Luna Concerts, and information on its Web site and product packaging.[16]

BT (British Telecom), one of the largest companies in the UK, recently added a key cause-related marketing partnership to make sure that youth are more empowered and have a greater voice in its communities. BT was determined to connect its charitable business services and customer outreach to impacting this issue—from making sure that no child in crisis goes unheard, to helping youth learn communication skills, and helping adults gain an increased appreciation of youth perspective. BT partnered with Childline, a national nonprofit that operates a youth crisis hotline (where every day approximately 4,000 children call, but due to a lack of capacity and funds, only 2,300 were getting through),[17] to revamp the call center technology, recruit volunteers from employees and customers, raise awareness of the help line, and raise money to fund its operations. BT has also developed family discussion workshops, helped fund youth councils, and championed the issue of youth voice with business and government leaders.[18]

Untouched World, a New Zealand–based environmentally and socially responsible wool apparel company, created a cause-related marketing relationship with the Blumine Island Project to raise awareness of this critical natural habitat and fund youth programs that conduct restoration projects combined with environmental education. Untouched World raises customer awareness through information in its retail and Web locations and raises funds by contributing to the project through its foundation.[19]

Developing a cause-related marketing program can run the risk of being perceived as mercenary or inauthentic. As we discussed in chapter 9, if you are not approaching a cause partnership for the right reasons (a real commitment to the cause and to a partnership that will truly advance the cause), don't bother. Getting into a cause-related partnership for the purpose of spin is a waste of time and money. While these partnerships can deliver real marketing value to companies, the strict return on investment for authentic partnerships is usually less than it is for other marketing tactics, and the potential downside from negative public relations is significant. However, if you are in it for the right reasons, and walk the talk on related issues, you can use the power of your voice to advance your values and legitimately advance market positioning, customer segment reach, and other marketing goals.

The Independent Sector's Mission & Market, the Cause Marketing Forum, and the Better Business Bureau offer resources and guidance for companies and nonprofits considering cause-related marketing programs.

When exploring a cause-related marketing partnership, ask yourself what causes naturally align with your company's values, what organizations impact these causes, what your company can offer that advances the cause (money, message reach, industry influence, etc.), what your potential partner can offer that advances your business goals, and what is your core motivation for pursuing the partnership. In general, an authentic cause-related partnership (when gauged by the AOM/ROI chart from chapter 3) will have very high AOM and reasonable ROI for the company, and very high AOM and ROI for the nonprofit partner.

Put Philanthropy at the Center of Your Value/Values Proposition

Kids today more often think of organic sandwich cookies (Newman-O's) and salad dressing than Butch Cassidy and Cool Hand Luke when they hear the name or see the face of Paul Newman. In addition to developing a very successful food products company, Newman has applied the company's full economic voice to creating a better world with his "all profits for charity" model. Newman's Own has donated over $200 million to thousands of educational and charitable causes.[20]

PeaceKeeper Cosmetics sells high-quality natural cosmetics and donates 100 percent of its profits to furthering peace, with a particular emphasis on international women's issues. The company is investing in exposing the international sex trade and helping women escape and build healthy lives.[21]

Social entrepreneurs and innovative nonprofit leaders have partnered with traditional entrepreneurs or started companies where 100 percent of the profits benefit a specific nonprofit as an earned income subsidiary. Sierra Club has an environmental mutual fund.[22] The Nature Conservancy works in partnership with Second Nature Software, a company created to publish and sell a wide variety of screen saver/desktop wallpaper collections and provide earnings to the Nature Conservancy and other nonprofit environmental organizations. Second Nature has contributed more than $2.5 million dollars to help preserve the world's natural wonders and wildlife.[23] The California Autism Foundation owns the San Francisco Chocolate Company, which offers employment to its clients and revenue to support its programs.[24]

While the various models of "all profits for charity" represent a small portion of socially responsible businesses, they demonstrate the strength of connecting the values of customers with their daily purchases. Whether your company has a charity-oriented product or you determine to share your expertise with the nonprofits you care about to bolster their earned income potential, remember that your company, your products, and your business skills can increase the resources available to causes that align with your mission.

Harness the Power of Business-to-Business Purchasing

We have commented throughout this book about customers voting with their dollars and making their purchasing decisions based upon both value and values. The same holds true for business purchasing. A powerful amplifier of your business's voice is the clear messages you send when you buy. When a company specifies to a vendor that it wants its materials printed on 100 percent postconsumer waste paper, it increases market demand for environmentally sustainable paper and sends a clear message to suppliers. Just as individuals seek fair trade products, organic food, and socially screened investments, socially responsible businesses can drive change through their purchasing.

Stephanie Odegard is an internationally recognized leader in contemporary rug design. She is founder and president of Odegard, Inc., a manufacturer, importer, and retailer of upscale and original designs of handmade Himalayan wool carpets made in Nepal. Her designs for high-end handmade rugs are distributed by over forty dealers worldwide and in her showrooms in New York, Washington, D.C., Chicago, Minneapolis, Miami, Zurich, London, and Milan. Stephanie's knowledge of the serious issues of child labor with many South East Asian manufacturers led to her exclusively sourcing suppliers that are certified to be free of any child labor. She and other designers and showrooms have partnered with Rugmark, which certifies its products as child labor free. Every Odegard carpet carries the Rugmark label.[25]

Pushpika Freitas created MarketPlace: Handwork of India to increase sustainable employment and economic security for women in India. MarketPlace collaborates with women-owned cooperatives to develop and produce apparel and gift items. Besides striving to provide economic security, MarketPlace seeks to empower women, through running their own businesses to having a voice in decisions concerning themselves, their children, and their communities. MarketPlace sells through its own catalog and Web site and at select retailers, increasing the incomes and economic independence of its suppliers.[26]

Pacific Natural Foods is one of America's largest producers of organic packaged broths, soups, and nondairy beverages. It sources ingredients from farmers who share its deep commitment to organic and sustainable farming and has even invested in establishing its own farms and ranches.[27]

Many socially responsible companies make extra efforts to source from local suppliers, assure that minority- and women-owned businesses are fairly represented in their supply chain, and include environmental and social considerations in their purchasing policies and decisions. The use of your business's economic voice can influence suppliers, educate customers, and ultimately change the behavior of markets.

Use the Power of Your Voice to Change the World

Socially responsible businesses by their nature are forces for change. By making purposeful choices about how and when to use the power of your business's voice, you increase your impact and influence and better advance your mission.

To use the power of your voice to change the world, ask yourself a few questions:

- Does our core business proposition leverage our communication to advance our values?

- Are we using the power of our communication and marketing tools to amplify the voices of others (customers, nonprofit partners, advocates, and activists) to advance values we care about?

- Do our business practices (hiring, promoting, supply chain, marketing, etc.) build the power of voice?

- Are we using communications assets to their maximum impact or are we wasting bandwidth by not using our packaging, Web sites, business locations, and other vehicles to also carry values messages?

- Are we aligning all the people and networks that we touch each day to causes/issues we care about, to our mission, and to our brand?

- Do our CSR, community, and philanthropic programs support and advance our voice about the issues we care about?

- Are we conscious about when we take a stand and when we don't? Are we clear about how we make these decisions, or do we let limited thinking and conventional wisdom tell us we cannot?

NEW SEASONS MARKET

LEVERAGE MARKETING FOR SOCIAL IMPACT

We have talked a great deal about New Seasons Market using the power of its voice to strengthen the regional organic and sustainable food economy. New Seasons often uses its voice by voting with its dollars to support regional suppliers, empowering its customers through information in its stores and online, and by establishing partnerships that promote environmental sustainability, organic agriculture, and access to healthy food.

On several occasions, New Seasons has taken a stand to support policy choices that were in accord with its values, often as a lone business or industry voice. One such issue has been support for country-of-origin labeling on produce. Many environmental, public health, and sustainable agriculture advocates support country-of-origin labeling. They believe that customers have a right to know where their food comes from and to be able to make informed purchasing choices. For some advocates, this issue is important due to the environmental impact of a tomato traveling further to the corner store than many students travel on a semester abroad. For others, this issue is important due to concerns about farming practices and pesticide use. Still others just want to be able to buy locally grown produce.

The majority of food retailers opposed the country-of-origin labeling regulations, expressing concerns about the expense of training staff, managing signs and labels, and the potential expense of implementation. New Seasons' Brian Rohter disagreed and spoke out, "Our customers have the right to know where their food comes from, our farm community needs country of origin legislation to help level the playing field against multinational industrialized farms, and we are already doing it so we know it is not too expensive or cumbersome."[28] New Seasons shared its point of view with policy makers, the media, employees, customers, and the community. It decided to take a stand to support its customers' rights, to further support its mission and brand promise, and because it recognized the power that a business voice (particularly from an industry opposed to a change) can have. In many small ways, New Seasons Market uses its voice to change the world.[29]

Business has unprecedented access and leverage to put issues on the table, empower communities and causes, educate customers, and influence policy makers. As a business leader, you can advance both your business's interests and your community vision by unleashing the power of your voice and using your business to amplify the voices of others who share your values. Whether you choose to take a stand on a policy issue, motivate change along your supply chain, or utilize the full bandwidth of your marketing tools to highlight an issue or cause, recognizing the full power of your voice, and of your marketing infrastructure, can make a difference. In fact, it can change the world. Your business offers you the opportunity to make marketing matter. We hope you will.

Epilogue

Writing this book has been an educational process. At the start, we were each aware of great work that was happening in the socially responsible business landscape. But we were surprised and inspired to discover how many companies—and visionary entrepreneurs—are using marketing in ways that matter. We both came to this project as marketer who love learning about customers and designing businesses to meet their needs and desires. And we both thought of our own companies as socially responsible businesses, knowing that social responsibility is a pathway to be traveled—not a final destination. Writing this book has led us to further examine our own businesses, to consider the ideas we have learned from other companies, and to ask ourselves, "Can this work in my company?" We come away even more convinced of the power and impact strategic marketing can have, particularly when combined with the discipline to communicate value and values and a desire to build lasting relationships.

The socially responsible business movement is changing the world. The social entrepreneurs we've written about, and thousands of others—including many of you reading this book—are revolutionizing business. You are harnessing the power of business to do much more than provide economic returns. From the democratization of capital to making political advocacy easy to ensuring that organic and healthy food is widely available to improving water and air quality—the products and services of socially responsible businesses have a positive impact on people, communities, and the environment. But we are still just scratching the surface of what is possible. As great as these examples may be, imagine a world where social responsibility and true accountability to a triple bottom line are the normative expectations of all business.

What would the world be like if 60 percent of America's invested assets were in socially responsible investments versus 9.4 percent?[1] How would the financial disparity between the haves and the have-nots change if every community had a ShoreBank? What would happen to childhood obesity and the health prospects of our nation if every school lunch were primarily organic? What would change in the quality of the air we breathe and the issue of climate change if purchasing an airline ticket also meant you were investing in new forests to offset pollution? What would be the impact on quality of life and family stability if all employees worked for companies whose minimum wage was a living wage?

What will it take for the socially responsible business movement to grow to scale and become simply the way business is done? We don't claim to have the answer. But we do believe that a contributing factor to creating this revolution is for all socially responsible businesses to use effective marketing. Doing so can bring socially responsible companies to scale. It can influence, encourage, and use the market to force mainstream businesses to adopt best practices. Strategic marketing can help us all become more effective storytellers—for our own companies and for the broader SRB community. It's a good story. And once known, it cannot be ignored. We believe it will inspire customers and communities to ask, "Why shouldn't I expect this from every business?"

We hope that the practices in *Marketing That Matters* will help increase your financial, social, and environmental results. Ultimately, we hope it will further cement the expectation that all businesses can make a profit and profit the community.

Notes

INTRODUCTION

1. "Best Places to Work in the Bay Area 2005," *San Francisco Business Times,* April 8, 2005.
2. Karen Post, "Once Upon a Brand: Part Two," *Fast Company,* March 2005, http://www.fastcompany.com/resources/marketing/post/032805.html (accessed February 22, 2006).

CHAPTER 1

1. Luna, "Our Story," Clif Bar Inc., http://www.lunabar.com/our_story/index.cfm?documentid=58 .html (accessed December 15, 2005).
2. Starre Vartan, "Soymilk Gets Fresh: Now Sold in Supermarkets, It May Put Dairy Cows Out of Business," *E: The Environmental Magazine,* September–October 2003 http://www.emagazine.com/view/?1131.html (accessed December 15, 2005).
3. Pam Stocks and John Turville, e-mail message to author, January 4, 2006.
4. Joleen Spencer, e-mail message to author, December 2, 2005.
5. Mary Houghton, phone interview by author, February 21, 2006.
6. Brian Rohter, interview by author, February 21, 2006.
7. Ibid.
8. Brian Rohter, e-mail message to author, February 13, 2006.

CHAPTER 2

1. Jeff Mendelsohn, e-mail message to author, February 13, 2006.
2. Stonyfield Yogurt, "About Us," Stonyfield Farm, http://www.stonyfield.com/AboutUs/.
3. Joleen Spencer, e-mail message to author, December 2, 2005.
4. Ron Grzywinski, phone interview by author, February 21, 2006.
5. Steve Smith, e-mail message to author, January 25, 2006.
6. Joleen Spencer, e-mail message to author, December 2, 2005.
7. Brian Rohter, interview by author, February 21, 2006.
8. Brian Rohter, e-mail message to author, February 13, 2006.

CHAPTER 3

1. Ron Grzywinski, phone interview by author, February 21, 2006.
2. Joleen Spencer, e-mail message to author, February 24, 2006.
3. Nina Smith, e-mail message to author, February 9, 2006.
4. Brian Rohter, e-mail message to author, February 13, 2006.
5. Jeff Mendelsohn, e-mail message to author, February 13, 2006.
6. Joleen Spencer, e-mail message to author, February 24, 2006.
7. Flexcar, "Vision," Mobility, Inc., http://www.flexcar.com/vision/default.asp (accessed February 15, 2006).
8. Susan Burns, "Keeping Our Eye on the Goal—How to Measure Corporate Sustainability Progress," *Natural Strategies,* March 2000, http://naturalstrategies.com/publications/sb_epis.pdf (accessed December 17, 2005).
9. Jennifer Bogo, "Business Savvy: Making Room on the Shelves for a New Generation of Greener Goods," *E: The Environmental Magazine,* July–August 2000, http://www.emagazine.com/view/?297.html (accessed December 15, 2005).
10. Jason Graham-Nye, e-mail message to author, February 14, 2006.
11. Joleen Spencer, e-mail message to author, February 24, 2006.
12. Nadine Thompson, phone interview by author, December 28, 2005; and e-mail message to author, March 6, 2006.
13. Joleen Spencer, e-mail message to author, February 24, 2006.
14. Jason Graham-Nye, e-mail message to author, February 14, 2006.
15. Jeff Mendelsohn, e-mail message to author, February 13, 2006.
16. Stonyfield Yogurt—Moos Releases, "Stonyfield Farm Converts Best-Selling Fat Free Line of Quart Yogurts to Organic," Stonyfield Farm, http://www.stonyfield.com/AboutUs/ MoosReleases_ Display.cfm?pr_id=65 (accessed December 6, 2005).
17. Brian Rohter, interview by author, February 21, 2006.
18. Brian Rohter, e-mail message to author, February 13, 2006.

CHAPTER 4

1. Ben Cohen and Jerry Greenfield, *Ben & Jerry's Double-Dip: Lead with Your Values and Make Money, Too* (New York: Fireside, 1997).
2. Gabe Luna-Ostaseski, e-mail message to author, September 9, 2005.

3. Mark Henricks, "5 Best Customer Service Ideas," *Entrepreneur Magazine,* March 1999, http://www.entrepreneur.com/article/ 0,4621,229932,00.html (accessed December 15, 2005).

4. Abraham Maslow, *Toward a Psychology of Being* (New York: John Wiley & Sons, 1968).

5. Ibid.

6. Douglas Atkin, *The Culting of Brands: When Customers Become True Believers* (New York: Portfolio, 2004).

7. Pete Blackshaw, "The Pocket Guide to Consumer Generated Media," editorial, *ClickZ,* June 28, 2005, http://www.clickz.com/ experts/brand/cmo/article.php/3515576 (accessed August 26, 2005).

8. Danny Grossman, phone interview by author, August 26, 2005; and Wild Planet Toys, Inc., "About Us," http://www.wildplanet .com/aboutus/index.php (accessed August 26, 2005).

9. Eric Ryan, phone interview by author, August 22, 2005; and Method Products, Inc., "About method," http://www.method home.com/about (accessed August 22, 2005).

10. Ray Anderson, *Mid-Course Correction: Toward a Sustainable Enterprise: The Interface Model* (Atlanta: Peregrinzilla Press, 1999).

11. Ibid.

12. Chip DeGrace, phone interview by author, August 30, 2005; and Interface FLOR, http://www.interfaceflor.com.

13. Brian Rohter, interview by author, February 21, 2006.

14. Brian Rohter, e-mail message to author, February 13, 2006.

CHAPTER 5

1. "A Wal-Mart for the Granola Crowd: John Mackey Sees No Limit to the Appetite for Natural Foods," *The Economist,* July 30, 2005, http://economist.com/people/displaystory .cfm?story_id=4222115.

2. Ibid.

3. W. Chan and Renée Mauborgne, "How Southwest Airlines Found a Route to Success," *London Financial Times,* May 13, 1999, http://www.insead.edu/kim/newspparticles/FT/FT130599 .htm (accessed October 12, 2005).

4. C.K. Prahalad and Stuart L. Hart, *The Fortune at the Bottom of the Pyramid: Eradicating Poverty Through Profits* (New Jersey: Wharton School, 2005).

5. Ibid.

6. Hewlett-Packard, "HP e-Inclusion," http://www.hp.com/
   e-inclusion/en/index.html (accessed October 10, 2005).

7. U.S. Census Bureau, http://www.census.gov/Press-Release/www/
   releases/archives/cb05ff-14-3.pdf (accessed December 15, 2005).

8. Charles Fishman, "The Anarchist's Cookbook," *Fast Company*,
   July 2004, http://www.fastcompany.com/magazine/84/wholefoods
   .html (accessed October 12, 2005).

9. Andrew Freeman, phone interview by author, August 25, 2005.

10. Ibid.

11. Ibid.

12. Kimpton Hotels, "Annual Red Ribbon Campaign," http://www
    .kimptonhotels.com/cares_redribbon.aspx (accessed August 25,
    2005).

13. Kimpton Hotels, "Diversity News," http://www.kimptonhotels
    .com/diversity_news.aspx (accessed August 25, 2005).

14. Ben Cohen and Jerry Greenfield, *Ben & Jerry's Double-Dip:
    Lead with Your Values and Make Money, Too* (New York:
    Fireside, 1997).

15. Joleen Spencer, e-mail message to author, February 24, 2006.

16. Jeff Sabatini, "2006 Lexus RX 400h: The Hybrid Emperor's
    New Clothes," *New York Times*, July 31, 2005.

17. Brian Rohter, interview by author, February 21, 2006.

18. Brian Rohter, e-mail message to author, February 13, 2006.

CHAPTER 6

1. Carolyn Said, "Entrepreneurs Hear That Green Is Trendy
   Way To Go: Co-Op America Conducts 3-Day Conference,"
   San Francisco Chronicle, November 3, 2005.

2. William Baue, "Shifting the Sustainability Dialogue from Values
   to Value," Social Funds, http://www.socialfunds.com/news/
   article.cgi/article920.html (accessed November 9, 2005).

3. Nat Worden, "Discounting Growth at Walmart, Target," The
   Street, May 11, 2005, http://www.thestreet.com/_googlen/
   markets/natworden/10222734.html (accessed November 9, 2005).

4. Jon Entine, "Body Shop's Packaging Starts to Unravel,"
   Australian Financial Review, December 18, 2002, http://www
   .jonentine.com/reviews/Body_Shop_AFR.htm (accessed
   November 2, 2005).

5. Edelman Study, "Talking from the Inside Out: The Rise of
   Employee Bloggers," Network World, http://www.networkworld
   .com/details/7586.html (accessed December 10, 2005).

6. Ryan Mathews and Fred Crawford, *The Myth of Excellence* (New York: Three Rivers Press, 2003).

7. Steve Ballou, Julian Chu, and Gina Paglucia Morrison, "Deeper Customer Insight," IBM Business Consulting Services, http://www1.ibm.com/services/ondemand/business/deeper_insights.html (accessed November 2, 2005).

8. Ibid.

9. gDiapers, "gDiapers 101," http://www.gdiapers.com/gdiapers101 (accessed November 8, 2005).

10. Kim Graham-Nye, phone interview by author, November 8, 2005.

11. Seventh Generation, "About Us," http://www.seventhgeneration.com/about_us (accessed November 12, 2005).

12. Procter & Gamble, "Company," http://www.pg.com/company/index/jhtml (accessed November 12, 2005).

13. Seventh Generation, "About Us: Operating Principles," http://www.seventhgeneration.com/about_us/operating.php (accessed May 22, 2006).

14. "General Mills' Box Tops Promo Hits In-store Bakeries," *Progressive Grocer,* October 5, 2005.

15. David W. Norton, "Toward Meaningful Brand Experiences," *Design Management Journal,* Winter 2003.

16. Rob Walker, "P.C. Tea," *New York Times Magazine,* July 3, 2005.

17. Ibid.

18. Douglas Atkin, *The Culting of Brands* (New York: Portfolio, 2004).

19. Danielle Sacks, "It's Easy Being Green," *Fast Company,* August 2004, http://www.fastcompany.com/magazine/85/aveda.html (accessed October 5, 2005).

20. Alison Overholt, "The Good Earth," *Fast Company,* December 2003, http://www.fastcompany.com/magazine/77/goodearth.html (accessed October 5, 2005).

21. Brian Rohter, interview by author, February 21, 2006.

22. Brian Rohter, e-mail message to author, February 13, 2006.

CHAPTER 7

1. Gary Erickson, *Raising the Bar: The Story of Clif Bar Inc.* (San Francisco: Jossey-Bass, 2004).

2. Cathy Keen, "Americans More Likely to Let Their Emotions Do the Buying," University of Florida, August 1, 2002, http://www.napa.ufl.edu/2002news/ademotions.htm (accessed October 5, 2005).

3. Kevin Roberts, *Lovemarks* (New York: Powerhouse Books, 2004).

4. Pamela Paul, "Sell It to the Psyche," "Inside Business," Bonus Section, *Time*, October 2003.

5. Marc Gobe, *Emotional Branding* (New York: Allworth Press, 2001).

6. Naomi Klein, *No Logo* (New York: Picador, 2002).

7. Aron Shields, "Should It Be Up to the Brand Owner to Tell the Truth?" Brandchannel.com, February 2, 2003, http://www.brandchannel.com/view_comments.asp?dc_id=26 (accessed November 25, 2005).

8. Karen Post, "Once Upon a Brand: The Top 10 Brand Story-tellers," *Fast Company*, February 2005, http://www.fastcompany.com/resources/marketing/post/022105_dblclk.html (accessed November 26, 2005).

9. George Silverman, *The Secrets of Word of Mouth Marketing* (New York: Amacom, 2001).

10. Putumayo, "About Us," http://www.putumayo.com (accessed November 17, 2005).

11. Ethos Water, "About Ethos," http://www.ethoswater.com (accessed November 5, 2005).

12. Faiza Elmasry, "Water for a Thirsty World," *Voice of America News*, August 17, 2005, http://www.utexas.edu/conferences/africa/ads/1020.html (accessed November 15, 2005).

13. Jim Donald, "Starbucks Buys Philanthropic Water Company," BevNet.com, April 12, 2005, http://www.bevnet.com/news/2005/04-12-2005-Starbucks_Water_Ethos_Jim%20Donald.asp (accessed November 15, 2005).

14. Kevin Roberts, *Lovemarks* (New York: Powerhouse Books, 2004).

15. Ibid.

16. Socially Responsible Marketing, "Case Histories," http://www.sociallyresponsiblemarketing.com/hasbro.html (accessed November 10, 2005).

17. Shelly Strom, "Tazo Tea Uses Connections to Become Branding Case Study," *Portland Business Journal*, June 29, 2001, http://www.bizjournals.com/portland/stories/2001/07/02/story5.html (accessed November 10, 2005).

18. Vivean Manning-Schaffel, "Zen and the Art of Brand Maintenance," Brandchannel.com, April 4, 2005, http://www.brandchannel.com/features_effect.asp?pf_id=257 (accessed November 11, 2005).

19. Ibid.

20. Yves Behar, phone interview by author, December 5, 2005; and http://www.birkenstockusa.com (accessed December 6, 2005).

21. Brian Rohter, interview by author, February 21, 2006.

22. Brian Rohter, e-mail message to author, February 13, 2006.

CHAPTER 8

1. Kevin A. Clark, *Brandscendence: Three Essential Elements of Enduring Brands* (Chicago: Dearborn Trade, 2004).

2. Douglas Atkin, *The Culting of Brands* (New York: Portfolio, 2004).

3. Melanie Wells, "Cult Brands," Forbes.com, April 16, 2001, http://www.forbes .com/ forbes/2001/0416/198_print.html (accessed December 6, 2005).

4. Laura Cummings, "Business Reporter," BBC News Online, July 9, 2003, http://news.bbc.co.uk/1/hi/business/3014477.stm (accessed December 6, 2005).

5. Patagonia, "About Patagonia," http://www.patagonia.com/about/main_about_us.shtml (accessed December 5, 2005).

6. Yvon Chouinard, *Let My People Go Surfing: The Education of a Reluctant Businessman* (New York: Penguin, 2005).

7. Patagonia, "About Patagonia," http://www.patagonia.com/about/main_about_us .shtml (accessed December 5, 2005).

8. Yvon Chouinard, *Let My People Go Surfing: The Education of a Reluctant Businessman* (New York: Penguin, 2005).

9. Ibid.

10. "How Patagonia Uses Word of Mouth Marketing (Instead of Traditional Campaigns)," Marketing Sherpa, March 8, 2004, http://library.marketingsherpa.com/barrier.cfm?CID=2625 (accessed on September 6, 2005).

11. Ben McConnell and Jackie Huba, *Creating Customer Evangelists: How Loyal Customers Become A Volunteer Sales Force* (Chicago: Dearborne Trade, 2003).

12. Phillip Britt, "Online Banking Clicks with Customers," *CRM Magazine,* November 18, 2004, http://www.destinationcrm .com/articles/default.asp?ArticleID=4636&ml=3 (accessed December 10, 2005).

13. George Silverman, "How to Harness the Awesome Power of Word of Mouth," Marketing Navigation, Inc., http://www .mnav.com/H2Harnwom.htm (accessed November 6, 2005).

14. Danielle Sacks, "Fast Talk: Brands We Love: Luna Bar: Start a Movement," *Fast Company,* August 4, 2004, http://www

.fastcompany.com/magazine/85/fasttalk.html (accessed
November 6, 2005).

15. Suzanne Vranica, "Marketer's New Idea: Get the Consumer to
Design the Ads," *Wall Street Journal,* December 13, 2005.

16. Brian Rohter, interview by author, February 21, 2006.

17. Brian Rohter, e-mail message to author, February 13, 2006.

CHAPTER 9

1. Jeffrey Hollender, e-mail message to author, February 12, 2006.

2. Rainforest Alliance, "Profiles in Sustainable Agriculture: Chiquita
Reaps a Better Banana," http://www.rainforest-alliance.org/
programs/profiles/chiquita.html (accessed December 15, 2006).

3. Ibid.

4. Jason Graham-Nye, e-mail message to author, February 14, 2006.

5. Joleen Spencer, e-mail message to author, February 24, 2006.

6. John Emrick, interview by author, December 20, 2006; and
Derek Smith, e-mail message to author, December 29, 2005.

7. Jeffrey Hollender, e-mail message to author, February 12, 2006.

8. Brian Rohter, e-mail message to author, February 13, 2006.

9. BSD Global, "Case Study: Nike," International Institute for Sustainable Development, http://www.bsdglobal.com/viewcasestudy
.asp?id=81 (accessed December 15, 2005).

10. The Natural Step, "Update: Nike Launches Sustainability Inte-
gration Initiative," http://www.naturalstep.org/learn/docs/misc/
nikelaunchesinitiative.pdf (accessed January 3, 2006).

11. BSD Global, "Case Study: Nike," International Institute for Sustainable Development, http://www.bsdglobal.com/viewcasestudy
.asp?id=81 (accessed December 15, 2005).

12. Judy Wicks, e-mail message to author, February 11, 2006.

13. Michelle Peterman, e-mail message to author, February 16, 2006.

14. Joleen Spencer, e-mail message to author, February 24, 2006.

15. National Service Inclusion Project, "Section VI: Access," http://
www.serviceandinclusion.org/handbook/index.php?page=section
vi (accessed February 21, 2006).

16. Amy Hall, e-mail message to author, February 13, 2006.

17. Joleen Spencer, e-mail message to author, February 24, 2006.

18. Flexcar, "Flexcar," Mobility, Inc., http://www.flexcar.com
(accessed April 25, 2006).

19. Jim Kelly, e-mail message to author, February 13, 2006.

20. Brian Rohter, interview by author, February 21, 2006.

21. Brian Rohter, e-mail message to author, February 13, 2006.

CHAPTER 10

1. Joleen Spencer, interview by author, February 24, 2006.
2. AlterNet, "A Media Monster Is Eating the Dems," Independent Media Institute, http://www.alternet.org/mediaculture/28478/ (accessed January 3, 2006).
3. Joleen Spencer, e-mail message to author, February 24, 2006.
4. Mariann Murphy, e-mail message to author, December 1, 2005.
5. Reggie Stanley, e-mail message to author, November 30, 2005.
6. Daniel Kadlec, "Amy Domini: Investing with a Conscience," *Time*, April 10, 2005, http://investmentvalues.biz/Articles/ TIME%20Magazine%20Archive%20Article%20—%20Amy% 20Domini%20—%20Apr_%2018,%202005.htm (accessed November 25, 2005).
7. Social Investment Forum, "Executive Summary," in *2005 Report on Socially Responsible Investing Trends in the United States,* Social Investment Forum, January 24, 2006.
8. Michael Kieschnick, e-mail message to author, February 27, 2006.
9. Stonyfield Farm, "On-Pack Messages to Support Health and Environmental Initiatives," http://www.stonyfield.com/Lids/index .cfm.
10. Self-Help, "Policy Initiatives," http://www.self-help.org/policy initiatives (accessed December 1, 2006).
11. Bruce Horovitz, "Marketing/Bruce Horovitz: Harmonic Convergence; Racial Tolerance Is Suddenly a Hot Topic in Advertising," *Los Angeles Times*, sec. D, January 19, 1993.
12. Beth Strachan, e-mail message to author, December 19, 2005.
13. Derek Smith, e-mail message to author, December 29, 2005.
14. Roey Thorpe, phone interview, December 19, 2005.
15. BreastCancer.org, "About Breast Cancer: Statistics," http://www .breastcancer.org/press_cancer_facts.html (accessed December 1, 2005).
16. Beth Strachan, e-mail message to author, December 19, 2005.
17. Childline, "Why Does Childline Need Your Support?" http://www.childline.org.uk/whyweneedyoursupport.html (accessed November 28, 2005).
18. Cause Marketing Forum, "Am I Listening? Campaign Overview," http://www.causemarketingforum.com/framemain .asp?ID=383 (accessed November 28, 2005).
19. Untouched World Foundation, "Vision," http://www.untouched world.com/en.uw/vision/foundation.htm (accessed November 20, 2005).

20. Newman's Own, "Common Good," http://www.newmansown .com/commongood.cfm (accessed November 21, 2005).
21. PeaceKeeper, "Who We Are," http://www.iamapeacekeeper .com/main/who_we_are.html (accessed November 21, 2005).
22. Sierra Club Mutual Funds, "Our Funds," Sierra Club, http://www.sierraclubfunds.com (accessed December 2, 2005).
23. David Manheart, phone interview by author, December 12, 2005.
24. John Clay, e-mail message to author, November 30, 2005.
25. Rugmark, "Stephanie Odegard: A Loom of One's Own," http://www.rugmark.org/odegard_importer_profile (accessed December 1, 2005).
26. Pushpika Freitas, e-mail message to author, December 1, 2005.
27. Pacific Natural Foods, "About Us," Pacific Foods of Oregon, Inc., http://www.pacificfoods.com/aboutus (accessed December 1, 2005); and Kevin Tisdale, e-mail message to author, March 6, 2006.
28. Brian Rohter, interview by author, February 21, 2006.
29. Brian Rohter, interview by author, February 13, 2006.

EPILOGUE

1. Executive Summary, *2005 Report on Socially Responsible Investing Trends in the United States*, Social Investment Forum, January 24, 2006.

Index

About Social Venture Network

SVN transforms the way the world does business by connecting, leveraging, and promoting a global community of leaders for a more just and sustainable economy.

Since its founding in 1987, SVN has grown from a handful of visionary individuals into a vibrant community of 400 business owners, investors, and nonprofit leaders who are advancing the movement for social responsibility in business. SVN members believe in a new bottom line for business, one that values healthy communities and the human spirit as well as high returns.

As a network, SVN facilitates partnerships, strategic alliances, and other ventures that promote social and economic justice. SVN compiles and promotes best practices for socially responsible enterprises and produces unique conferences that support the professional and personal development of business leaders and social entrepreneurs.

Please visit http://www.svn.org for more information on SVN membership, initiatives, and events.

About the Authors

Chip Conley is founder and CEO of Joie de Vivre Hospitality, Northern California's largest hotelier. Chip has won numerous awards, including Guerrilla Marketer of the Year from the American Travel Marketing Executives, Northern California Entrepreneur of the Year, National Humanitarian Hospitality Company of the Year, and the Experience Stager of the Year. He is the author of *The Rebel Rules: Daring to Be Yourself in Business* and *Business Rules of Thumb* (with Seth Godin). His next book, *Peak,* will be available in September 2007.

Eric Friedenwald-Fishman is president and creative director of Metropolitan Group, one of the country's leading full-service strategic communication and social marketing agencies with offices in Portland, Oregon; Chicago; and Washington, D.C. Eric has developed brands and marketing strategies for many well-known socially responsible businesses. Eric is particularly passionate about harnessing marketing to drive social change and is the primary author of the Public Will Building Framework, a strategic communication approach to creating sustainable social change.

Values-Driven Business: How to Change the World,
Make Money, and Have Fun
by Ben Cohen and Mal Warwick
This short, easy-to-read book details every step in the process of
creating and managing a small or midsized business that will reflect your personal values, not force you to hide them. As co-
founder of the immensely successful Ben & Jerry's Homemade
Ice Cream, Ben Cohen is one of the best-known examples of personal integrity and social commitment in the business community. Social Venture Network chair Mal Warwick is the leader of
one of the world's oldest and most respected organizations committed to building a just and sustainable world through business. Using down-to-earth language and abundant examples,
they combine their decades of experience to show how virtually
any small business can be efficient, competitive, and successful
while pursuing a "triple bottom line" of profit, people, and
planet.
*February 2006, $12.00, paperback. ISBN 978-1-57675-358-3 or
1-57675-358-1*

True to Yourself: Leading a Values-Based Business
by Mark Albion
This is an engaging, accessible guide to a critical component of
socially responsible business: effective leadership. Mark Albion,
author of the *New York Times* bestseller *Making a Life, Making a Living,* argues that small-business leaders concerned with
more than the bottom line are not only more fulfilled but also
more successful with more sustainable lives. He uses real-world
examples to identify the qualities and specific practices of small-
business leaders who combine profit with purpose, margin with

mission, value with values. Whether you're just starting out or many years on your way, *True to Yourself* will help you to get and stay on track.

July 2006, $12.00, paperback, ISBN 978-1-57675-378-1 or 1-57675-378-6

Growing Local Value: How to Build Business Relationships That Strengthen Your Community
by Laury Hammel and Gun Denhart

This down-to-earth guide explains how to build or expand a values-driven business that is deeply embedded in the life of the local community. While most people think of community engagement only in terms of philanthropy or volunteerism, entrepreneurs Laury Hammel and Gun Denhart show how every aspect of a business (from product creation to employee recruitment to vendor selection to raising capital) holds the dual promise of bigger profits and a stronger local community. Including practical tools such as a Community Involvement Self-Assessment, *Growing Local Value* explores the full spectrum of ways in which a business can contribute to its community—and the benefits it receives when it does.

November 2006, $12.00, paperback, ISBN 978-1-57675-371-2 or 1-57675-371-9

**For more information, check out the
Social Venture Network Series Web page:
www.svnbooks.com.**

About Berrett-Koehler Publishers

Berrett-Koehler is an independent publisher dedicated to an ambitious mission: Creating a World That Works for All.

We believe that to truly create a better world, action is needed at all levels—individual, organizational, and societal. At the individual level, our publications help people align their lives with their values and with their aspirations for a better world. At the organizational level, our publications promote progressive leadership and management practices, socially responsible approaches to business, and humane and effective organizations. At the societal level, our publications advance social and economic justice, shared prosperity, sustainability, and new solutions to national and global issues.

A major theme of our publications is "Opening Up New Space." They challenge conventional thinking, introduce new ideas, and foster positive change. Their common quest is changing the underlying beliefs, mind-sets, institutions, and structures that keep generating the same cycles of problems, no matter who our leaders are or what improvement programs we adopt.

We strive to practice what we preach—to operate our publishing company in line with the ideas in our books. At the core of our approach is *stewardship,* which we define as a deep sense of responsibility to administer the company for the benefit of all of our "stakeholder" groups: authors, customers, employees, investors, service providers, and the communities and environment around us.

We are grateful to the thousands of readers, authors, and other friends of the company who consider themselves to be part of the "BK Community." We hope that you, too, will join us in our mission.

Be Connected

Visit Our Website

Go to www.bkconnection.com to read exclusive previews and excerpts of new books, find detailed information on all Berrett-Koehler titles and authors, browse subject-area libraries of books, and get special discounts.

Subscribe to Our Free E-Newsletter

Be the first to hear about new publications, special discount offers, exclusive articles, news about bestsellers, and more! Get on the list for our free e-newsletter by going to www.bkconnection.com.

Participate in the Discussion

To see what others are saying about our books and post your own thoughts, check out our blogs at www.bkblogs.com.

Get Quantity Discounts

Berrett-Koehler books are available at quantity discounts for orders of ten or more copies. Please call us toll-free at (800) 929-2929 or email us at bkp.orders@aidcvt.com.

Host a Reading Group

For tips on how to form and carry on a book reading group in your workplace or community, see our website at www.bkconnection.com.

Join the BK Community

Thousands of readers of our books have become part of the "BK Community" by participating in events featuring our authors, reviewing draft manuscripts of forthcoming books, spreading the word about their favorite books, and supporting our publishing program in other ways. If you would like to join the BK Community, please contact us at bkcommunity@bkpub.com.